The Five Warrior Virtues

American Agoge Project

Honor Integrity Loyalty Temperance Courage

Blacksmith Publishing

founded 2013

The Five Warrior Virtues

A Practical Philosophy for the American Fighting Man

Paul D. LeFavor

"A soldier, full of strange oaths and bearded like the pard, jealous in honor, sudden and quick in quarrel, seeking the bubble reputation even in the cannon's mouth." – Shakespeare

The Five Warrior Virtues: A Practical Philosophy for
the American Fighting Man

by Paul D. LeFavor

Copyright © 2023 by Blacksmith Publishing

ISBN 9781956904130

Printed in the United States of America

Published by Blacksmith LLC
Fayetteville, NC

www.Blacksmithpublishing.com

Direct inquiries and/or orders to the above web address.

Contents

For my father, David LeFavor.
A man of great worth.

Foreword

What is a warrior? Going to my dictionary, I find "an aggressive person experienced in fighting" while another dictionary attempts to improve on the definition by adding, "one who is engaged enthusiastically in an activity, cause, or conflict." Still not satisfied, I decide to elicit assistance from a legendary warrior from my childhood memory, Sitting Bull, who states, "a warrior is one who sacrifices himself for the good of others, to care for the elderly, the defenseless, and above all, children." Perhaps because of time I spent serving in the military, I also imagine a warrior to be like Leonidas's 300 hoplites standing firm at the Battle of Thermopylae, willing to die for honor. However, I also realize there's no need to limit my search to history or antiquity for an answer, able to recall significant instances in my own life where I've personally witnessed the actions of warriors that had nothing to do with something as glorious as defending the Gates of Greece. Therefore, I believe to better understand what IS a warrior, I must discover what it is that MAKES a warrior. I must ascertain the essence of what motivates an individual to take action that ultimately bestows upon him the cherished accolade, warrior, or more specifically, American Warrior.

In our country, like so many other places around the world, our values, beliefs, and principles are passed along to the next generation of men through three primary avenues. These are family, faith, and community. Within our communities, various organizations are created to assist families with reinforcing fundamental values and basic religious beliefs and to teach important primal tasks and activities that help develop young boys become productive men, husbands, and fathers. One such organization that comes to mind is the Boy Scouts of America (BSA). From its inception in 1910, the Boy Scouts of America sought to foster an environment that would produce abled-bodied young men who would make excellent citizens and warriors. For over a century, it has been a stated goal of the Scouts to produce warriors. The 1967 Boy Scout's Handbook included the words,

Have you ever dreamed of hiking the wilderness trails that were worn down under moccasins hundreds of years ago? Do you hear in your imagination the almost soundless dip-dip of Indian canoe paddles or the ring of the ax of an early pioneer hewing a home out of the American wilderness? Have you followed with your mind's eye the covered wagons on the trek across our continent? Have you thought of the men and women who built our country by their determination and devotion? You are the descendant of those people. You are the guardian of what they built. You are the American on whom the future of our wonderful country depends. Today you are an American boy. Before long you will be an American man. It is important to America and to yourself that you become a citizen of fine character, physically strong, mentally awake, and morally straight.

As a boy, I loved scouting. I started out as a Cub Scout probably around age six, then progressed on through the Webelos when I got a little older, always working hard to complete various tasks to fill my shirt with those coveted badges. Eventually I reached middle school and was able to become a full-fledged Boy Scout. I have lots of fond memories of my many years in scouting. I learned many camping and life skills that helped form me into the man I am today. Afterall, that was the mission of the Boy Scouts, making men out of boys. Sadly, the Boy Scouts became a magnet for pedophiles and eventually were forced to file for bankruptcy after shelling out millions of dollars in lawsuits over leaders sexually abusing boys. After hemorrhaging millions of dollars, the Boy Scouts of America took the radical step of including girls in its membership in a last-ditch effort to save the organization. Unfortunately, the original mission of the Boy Scouts of America no longer exists.

What was best in the Boy Scouts of America program was that it mirrored that of the ancient Spartan Agoge. The Agoge was the name of the school mandated for all Spartan males beginning at the age of seven and ending at age twenty-one. "Agoge" literally means 'guidance' or 'training.' This training regimen encompassed every domain of human interaction in its social, political, emotional, physical, and spiritual components. It emphasized military training, hunting, social skills, and loyalty to the nation and its principles. The overall goal of this system of excellence was the creation of a Spartan man who could serve as a citizen and warrior. The importance of the Agoge cannot be overstated as it was this ancient system that produced Leonidas and his 300. Arguably then, it was the Agoge that saved the western world from enslavement.

As it is said, the most powerful thing is an idea whose time has come. The mission of the American Agoge

Foreword

Project (AAP) is to foster an environment that produces able-bodied men of fine character that will make excellent citizen-warriors. Fine character and able-bodied is thus defined as physically and spiritually strong, mentally focused, morally straight, and socially astute. The American Agoge Project exists to help American boys become the kind of men that possess such qualities. This project exists to promote three values: man, God-fearing, and warrior. By valuing "man," we mean the qualities of manhood that have fallen prey to a complex set of socially conditioned, media-stimulated woke agendas. Such qualities that are denigrated, yet vital to the future success of the family, and our Country. Central to this project is the value of a man who fears God and hates evil. And warrior, is the class of men who answer the call of duty, to serve in the ranks with those who defend our lives and liberties. In valuing these noble qualities, the goal is to enable the mind and body preparation for the American Warrior Class. The American Agoge Project is an idea whose time has come.

This book, which is the ground floor of this project, seeks to codify the five warrior virtues that form the foundation of every warrior code, in every nation, of every age. Any discussion of these virtues will therefore be either recovery or discovery. Both are good.

Michael Blackburn
co-Founder
Blacksmith Publishing
American Agoge Project

Preface: A Christian Apology

As it has been said, nothing justifies the writing of prefaces, except that they are in fact epilogues. That is, they are written last and serve as a vehicle for those general observations one feels inclined to make regarding the scope and nature of the whole book. This preface was written last and gives voice to the subtext, or metanarrative of this book.

Many soldiers believe that serving in war somehow places them outside the bounds of God's grace. We have an occasion in holy writ that demonstrates precisely that sentiment. In Luke chapter three, John the Baptist is on his mission to prepare the way of the Lord. In doing so, he is preaching, giving knowledge of salvation, in the remission of sins, and baptizing in the Jordan River. The people ask what they should do to bear fruit worthy of repentance. John replies, "He who has two tunics, let him give to him who has none," and so on.

Then some soldiers came down to be baptized. Naturally, they likewise asked John, "And what should we do?" The soldiers' question reflects a prevalent fear of many soldiers that they are beyond God's grace because, as they suppose, God seemingly disapproves of their occupation. The words they use, "even us?" reflects this. John's reply to them is threefold: "Do not intimidate anyone or accuse falsely, and be content with your wages." With this reply, the first thing we learn is the pursuit of your calling as a soldier is not incompatible with your Christian faith. Notice, John did not say: Quit soldiering. Likewise, the Apostle Paul teaches in 1 Corinthians 7:24: "Let each one remain with God in that state in which he was called." Correlating these truths, we may say: Remain in your calling, and see to it that you serve God honorably in it. That is what the Lord expects out of us all. To serve with honor.

By way of a Christian apology, Greek for "defense," I want to take a brief look at what John the Baptist says to these soldiers. There is much there. First, John has something to tell us about authority. He says, "Do not intimidate anyone." What he means is, when you serve your country in the military, don't abuse the authority delegated to you. Now, this speaks volumes to us as soldiers. As the Scripture teaches, the State has the delegated authority from God to punish anyone who threatens the safety and the order of society, whether those people are citizens involved in wrongdoing or whether they are powers from outside the state itself. For this reason, we obey the law and pay taxes. "Render to Caesar the things that are Caesar's, and to God the things that are God's" (Mark 12:17). Caesar gets some of our coins. God is to get our lives and our best. God is sovereign over human affairs, including government. Thus, we honor God by honoring the government He has put in place. A sober reading of Romans 13:1-7 will make this clear.

In light of this, "Do not intimidate anyone," is another way of saying, don't abuse the power of the sword delegated to you. That is, the sword is never to be used as an instrument of hate. War, in the protection and vindication of justice, is not to be prompted by hate but by the love of justice. Such love never contradicts the love of our enemies. Whenever a soldier uses weapons of war as instruments of personal vengeance, the dictates of both justice and love have been desecrated. As a soldier, use your sword for justice and not for evil. Another thought. Soldiers that are immature and unsure of themselves often try to exert themselves to make up for their deficient qualities. "Do not intimidate anyone" is therefore a challenge to guard our hearts against using the authority delegated to us for personal gain. The Bible affords us many negative examples to avoid.

Fine, you say, but what of the Scripture which says, he who lives by the sword shall die by the sword? Context settles this difficult issue. Found in Mark 14, attempting to defend Jesus, and in a fit of rage, Peter draws his sword and most likely tries to cut a man's head off. Just in time, the man ducks out of the way of the swinging sword and loses his ear in the process. Then Jesus said to Peter, "Put your sword in its place, for all who take the sword will perish by the sword." Notice, this is not a command to throw away the sword, rather to put it in "its place." The sword has its place. Earlier, I mention Romans 13. In verse 4, the Apostle Paul declares, "Let every soul be subject to the governing authorities. For there is no authority except from God, and the authorities that exist are appointed by God." Paul goes on to describe a judge as one that bears the sword as a "minister of God."

In the context of Mark 14, as the events of Providence unfold, Jesus is going to be judged by God's ordained legitimate authority, despite the fact that this legitimate authority, the Sanhedrin, and the Roman proconsul, are misusing the power of the sword. If we step back and look, in this scene there are two swords, that of God's ordained legitimate authority, and that of Peter. In other words, in Luke 22, when Jesus tells His disciples of the coming need to have a sword, He recognized both the legitimate authority of the first sword, that of the government, and the potential need and place for the second, that of the individual. A sword of self-defense has its place.

Significantly, even then, Jesus did not command Peter to throw his sword away or surrender it. He simply said, "Put your sword in its place." Then, Jesus added that great accompanying principle: "For all who take the sword will perish by the sword." Some have misinterpreted this as a call for Christian pacifism, and that even self-defense is wrong. However, if you're a pacifist, you must be consistent in your position and say that all force is wrong. Therefore, if you are about to be raped you must not resist. If someone wants to kill you or your family when they break into your home, then you mustn't resist. You cannot call upon the justice of a government to execute someone who has killed your loved ones. You cannot resist in any way to such crimes. When it comes down to it, I doubt a true pacifist exists anywhere on the planet.

This is why I love knowing some biblical Greek. In the parallel passage of Matthew 26:52, Jesus declares, "For all who take the sword will perish by the sword." The word "take" is *lambano*, and here it's used as a participle, that is, an "ing" verb. In other words, those who are "taking up" the sword, and actively living by it, in a way that would characterize Peter when he was swinging it wildly, will die by it. Jesus says to His disciples, that's not to be the pattern of your life. You are to live by the Sword of the Lord, the Word of God; taking it up, and actively living by it. That is the way your life is to be characterized.

In light of this, this teaches us three things that highlight the importance of being spiritually minded: (1) Self-defense. Jesus told Peter to "Put your sword in its place." In other words, the sword used in defense has its place. (2) Submission to lawful authority. Jesus told Peter to "Put your sword in its place." In other words, the legitimate authority wielding the sword, is ordained by God, and is to be submitted to, as an expression of submission to God. (3) Spiritually minded. We are to live by the Spirit, and being spiritually minded, we may discern which situation we're in. The question is, which sword do we live by? There's a time for self-defense, and there's a time to submit to legitimate authority as an expression of our submission to the will of God. It's for this reason we sing, "It's not with swords loud clashing, nor roar of stirring drums, with deeds of love and mercy the heavenly kingdom comes." This is about balance and being spiritually minded.

Second, John has something to tell us about integrity. John says, "Don't accuse others falsely." Integrity is acting with honor and unwavering adherence to the commands of Scripture and conscience. Now why John says this is because accusing people falsely can lead to their imprisonment or wrongful death. As I will argue later, the word "integrity" comes to us from the Latin word "integer" and literally means "intact." This implies a lack of corruption or keeping one's morals intact. Integrity is hard to get and easy to lose, it must be safeguarded. It involves courting no man's favor, nor making decisions based on popularity, but rather seeking the will of God in every situation (Romans 12:2). "Do not accuse others falsely" is therefore a challenge to maintain your integrity even to your own hurt.

Third, John has something to tell us about possessions. He says, "Be content with your wages." As the Bible teaches, contentment is a mental and emotional state of satisfaction. In other words, contentment is a perspective. We have a great example from the Apostle Paul's imprisonment which he suffered for the gospel's sake. In his letter to the Philippians he writes, "I have learned in whatever state I am, to be content" (Philippians 4:11). The mighty apostle Paul had to learn how to be content! This doesn't come naturally. That means there's hope for you and I! Contentment doesn't come naturally, it's learned. And many times, it's relearned. Moreover, we often have to fight for it. Another thing Paul teaches us about contentment is that it's not according to our circumstances. He was writing the letter to the Philippian Church from a prison. He was in chains, without adequate clothing, and I imagine that the food wasn't all that good either. Happiness for most people is based on circumstances. But Paul said he learned to be content whatever the situation.

Moreover, contentment isn't comfort. Something every soldier knows, comforts come and go. Neither is contentment excitement. Excitement never lasts; it comes and goes. But contentment lasts after excitement is over. This is the nature of it. The best way to understand contentment is to consider its absolute antithesis which is covetousness. The Bible tells us that covetousness is idolatry because the contentment that the heart should be getting from God, it gets from something else. As John Calvin once put it, our hearts are idol factories. We can therefore be covetous of things like money, personal advancement, or honor. But unlike contentment, covetousness never gives us satisfaction. Like a mirage, covetousness leads us on an endless chase and never satisfies. Covetousness is contentment's kryptonite. It chokes the spiritual life out of us and gives rise to many other sins. It was for this reason Blaise Pascal once observed, "we prefer the chase to the quarry."

Being covetous caused the rich young ruler to turn away from Jesus. It caused the rich fool to deceive himself. The only antidote to covetousness is contentment. God's way of contentment comes by way of subtraction, not addition. John the Baptist outlined God's way of gaining contentment. He said, "He (that is Jesus) must increase, but I must decrease." Do you see?

Contentment is to be a deep-seated satisfaction. It's a sanctified perspective that what God provides is enough. This perspective is gained through decreasing ourselves and increasing Christ. On all levels. We have to guard our hearts against covetousness. Here's a prescription to serve Christ with honor: "Do not intimidate anyone or accuse falsely, and be content with your wages."

In light of this defense, let it be said, a good Christian never makes a bad soldier. Consider the fact that Jesus once remarked, "Not in all Israel have I found such great faith" (Matthew 8:10). The man Jesus spoke of was a Roman Centurion. As we seek to be the model soldiers in every formation, may the Lord enable us to serve with distinction for His glory and our good (Colossians 1:18).

Paul D. LeFavor
Camp Mackall
New Year's Day 2023

Introduction

Worthless males have always been detrimental to the safety, security, and survival of any State. During the times of the Judges in ancient Israel, the people were led by the high priest Eli. His tenure would be forever infamous due to his inability to discipline and restrain his wayward sons. Set apart to serve the Lord in the Tabernacle as priests, Eli's sons Hophni and Phineas instead served themselves. Their many transgressions included ingratiating themselves with the sacrifices offered to God. If this was not evil enough, they even had sex with the women who assembled at the Lord's Tabernacle.

They did these things because they neither knew God nor feared Him. Producing nothing and yet consuming everything, the Bible describes Hophni and Phineas as "worthless males" (1 Samuel 2:12). Eventually they were slaughtered, and Israel became subservient to their great enemy Philistia.

In America today, it is an undeniable fact that young men are failing. They're failing socially. A sustained attack on manhood and decades of political correctness have taken a toll telling young men that being masculine is toxic. Young men are told what *not* to do but never what they *should* do. Young men are failing educationally. Males are thirty percent more likely than girls to drop out or flunk out of school. On average, boys are lagging behind girls in math and a full grade level behind in English. One in four boys are categorized as having developmental disabilities. Beyond high school, 60% of students on college campuses are now women.

Young men are failing vocationally. As borne out by legions of findings, fewer young men are in the labor force, and more are opting to remain at home. They're simply failing to launch. According to Mike Rowe, America currently has roughly seven million able-bodied men sitting out of the work force. Skilled trades that have been traditionally performed by men, carpentry, electrician, plumbing, etc., are hemorrhaging workers. In fact, for every five men that leave the work force, only two enter.

No doubt the greatest factor in this death-spiral is the changing family dynamic. From the 1960-1990s, the percentage of children living apart for their biological father was 36%. It had been 17% in the 1950s. Today, it's estimated that HALF of all young men are growing up without a father. And what a tremendous effect this has had! A recent study of violent rapists found that 60% grew up without a father. Similarly tragic, a recent study found that of adolescents who committed homicides, 75% of them were likewise from fatherless homes. Statistics also show that children without fathers are three times more likely to drop out of school. I could go on.

In addition to the family dynamic, traditionally, the church, the school system, and one's community stood alongside the family to promote a culture that set boys on the right path for manhood. Tragically, as each of these buttressing elements that would normally promote traditional manhood have fallen prey to the feminist movement, political correctness, wokeness, in the last twenty years, we have witnessed a tremendous moral implosion, a lack of respect for authority, and a loss of basic manners. In short, without these mainstays of healthy culture, what we are now witnessing is unmitigated chaos, and pandemonium. As Václav Havel once mused, "What profound intellectual and moral impotence will the nation suffer tomorrow following the castration of culture today?"

Lacking good male role models, young men are also becoming lazy, and overweight. It's a known fact that one third of all young men today are clinically obese. Saying this negatively affects military recruitment would be an understatement. In light of this, the US military faces similar recruitment hurdles that it did after the Vietnam War. Albeit the problem is not merely a patriotic one as it's a physically fit one. The Army's goals for recruitment fell by 25% this year. Invariably, the military will be forced to keep lowering the standards to get people, which is decidedly the wrong answer.

Young men are also failing romantically. Lacking positive role models, and taking their cues from toxic ones, young men simply do not know how to behave around women. Instead, many see women as temporary, interchangeable sex objects. How this should concern women is voiced by Christina Hoff Sommers. In her book, *The War Against Boys*, she argues, these young men who are failing are "our sons; they are the people with whom our daughters will build a future. If our boys are in trouble, so are we all." In fact, Sommers goes as far to say, "We are turning against boys and forgetting a simple truth: that the energy, competitiveness, and corporal daring of normal, decent males is responsible for much of what is right in the world."[1]

In this confusing world of changing norms, young men are simply opting out of society. In their book, *Man Interrupted*, Philip Zimbardo and Nikita Coulombe identify various ways in which young men are withdrawing. The authors single out two salient issues, an addiction to video games and online porn. These two addictions, which offer alternate realities, and screen-based novelties, "have created a generation of shy, socially awkward, emotionally removed, and risk-adverse young men who are unable (and unwilling) to navigate the complexities and risks inherent to real-life relationships, school, and employment."[2]

According to the authors, the reason why young men are opting out is simple. They're retreating into an imaginary world where there is no rejection, and the objectives are clear, and they can control the outcomes. Producing nothing and yet consuming everything, American young men are therefore becoming worthless males.

---

[1] Christina Hoff Sommers, *The War Against Boys: How Misguided Policies are Harming Our Young Men* (New York: Simon & Schuster, 2015), 165.
[2] Philip Zimbardo and Nikita Coulombe, *Man, Interrupted: Why Young Men are Struggling & What We Can Do About It* (New York: Red Wheel, 2016), 329.

Introduction

All this is to say, the American man of today is in trouble. If there was ever needed a course correction for the demise of today's young men, it's now! This book is an attempt to do just that. There are many books that promote the warrior culture. This book is for the American fighting MAN. It is not meant to exclude women but seeks to bless them immeasurably so that they will benefit by the selfless service of strong men who are mature, masculine, and responsible. By masculine, it is meant not men who demand to be served, but rather men who serve and sacrifice for the good of others, including women.

This book is for the man who is called to serve in the ranks of America's warrior caste. Warfare is our domain. A short discussion on the profession of arms here will prove useful. Though it has been defined in romantic as well as scientific ways, at its best, if I may be permitted to say so, war exists to defend, amongst other things, the threatened independence of the state. As such, it is not an exact science, but rather, "a drama full of passion."[3] Or, to pay homage to Clausewitz, war is an extension of politics by other means. The Prussian general further broke down this thought in three ways.

First, he said that war is an instrument of policy. It's a political instrument that is to be controlled and shaped by policy.[4] Secondly, war is an act of violence to impose our

---

[3] Jomini, *The Art of War*, 12.
[4] Carl von Clausewitz, *On War*, Michael Howard and Peter Paret Translation (New York: Everyman's Library, 1993), Book I, Chapter 2, 102.

5

will on our enemy. War is therefore an act of violence. Thirdly, in what he referred to as "the climate of war," Clausewitz noted that war is the province of danger, the realm of uncertainty, the domain of physical exertion, and the sphere of chance. Putting it all together, in Clausewitz estimation, war is intrinsically violent, policy has a role in controlling and shaping it, and unseen causes dominate it. The way war is governed by these unseen forces, led Napoleon to observe, "The battlefield is a scene of constant chaos. The winner will be the one who controls that chaos, both his own and the enemies." World history has proven these philosophers of war to be correct. This is war in the abstract.

The military philosophers I mentioned made their assertions against the kind-hearted quaint beliefs of some people in their day, and ours, who think there's a way of disarming or defeating our enemy without bloodshed. In practice, war is like an immense terrible machine, organized by the blood-swollen Ares, the god of war himself.[5] Combat is an organized form of violence. Its immediate result is bloodshed, injury, suffering, and death. With its slain, war takes its invisible toll on the souls it touches, both that of combatants, along with their families and friends. Kind-hearted notions of humanity relegate such bold naked truths to the background. However quaint and hopeful, the reality of the world in which we live is not according to the pacifist's sentiment.

---

[5] Stephen Crane, *The Red Badge of Courage* (New York: Dover, 1990), 37.

Introduction

Likewise, it would be naive to overlook the fact that war is also a racket. America's most decorated general, Brigadier General Smedley Butler, once put it, "a racket is best described, I believe, as something that is not what it seems to the majority of people. Only a small "inside" group knows what it is about. It is conducted for the benefit of the very few, at the expense of the very many. Out of war a few people make huge fortunes."[6] As such, the huge profits are made by a small group of capitalist warmongers who remain safely at home. While these profiteers fill their coffers, those who serve are quartered and maimed by the hands of war. It's just the way it is. All veterans know it. Don't get me wrong. There are such things as "just wars." However, for the most part, Plato was right when he wrote, "all wars are due to the desire to acquire wealth."[7]

Because of this, and other weighty reasons which are beyond scope, invariably, there will be wars and rumors of wars until Doomsday. Don't misunderstand me. I'm not preaching a war spirit. I'm not saying, "give war a chance." In time of war, you can be sure politicians will dress up war in borrowed robes, preaching patriotism, love of Country and the like. As I will argue later, the best stance for the American warrior is to shoulder the task of defending freedom, without getting bogged down into politics, and without taking on what I would call a crusader mindset. That is, a belief that "God wills it." Suffice it to say I believe God tires of being called down

---

[6] Smedley D. Butler, *War is a Racket* (Port Townsend, WA: Feral House, 2003), 23.
[7] Plato, *Phaedo*.

on both sides of an argument. Mark Twain lampooned this phenomenon in his poem, *The War Prayer*:

O Lord our God, help us to tear their soldiers to bloody shreds with our shells; help us to cover their smiling fields with the pale forms of their patriot dead; help us to drown the thunder of the guns with the shrieks of their wounded, writhing in pain; help us to lay waste their humble homes with a hurricane of fire; help us to wring the hearts of their unoffending widows with unavailing grief; help us to turn them out roofless with their little children to wander unfriended the wastes of their desolated land.[8]

My simple point is this, when the thin veil of humanism is removed, along with its accompanying Pollyannish belief in an innate goodness of mankind, what you are left with is the utmost necessity to defend yourself and your countrymen from a world motivated by blind avarice, ferocity, lack of moral restraint, and an unchecked "will to power." The kind of warrior we need in this Country is the one who will defend our liberties, and deploy and engage our foes, even when it's not appreciated. Politics immaterial.

On a thought-provoking level, psychologist Norman Dixon states, war is energy: "In war, each side is kept busy turning its wealth into energy, which is then delivered, free, gratis and for nothing, to the other side. Such energy may be muscular, thermal, kinetic, or chemical. If, by means of, say, impossibly large funnels and gigantic reservoirs, they could capture and store the energy flung

---

[8] Mark Twain, *The War Prayer*.

at them by the other side, the recipients of this unsolicited gift would soon be so rich, and the other side so poor, that further warfare would be unnecessary for them and impossible for their opponents."[9]

All joking aside, history shows that nations that are not ready to defend their honor with arms decline and eventually fall. It was the reality of this view of the world that motivated and fortified America's warriors of the past to defend our lives and liberties for nearly 250 years. In light of that, this book seeks to codify the five warrior virtues that form the foundation of every warrior code, in every nation, of every age. These virtues that will be examined in depth are honor, integrity, loyalty, temperance, and courage. As will be argued, a concentrated focus and fostering of these virtues in America's fighting men will in turn help insure our Nation's future.

Kierkegaard once opined, "Life can only be understood backwards; but it must be lived forwards." I'm an Army veteran. From 1989-2009, I served twenty years, and was privileged to see a lot of the world and experience many things, including combat. Now that I'm in the afternoon of life, what I want to share I was never taught in a service school. To be sure, each school I was privileged to attend, the Ranger Course, the Special Forces Qualification Course, the Operator Training Course, and the like, taught me much regarding tactics, precision shooting, leadership, and myself, albeit none offered a warrior

---

[9] Norman F. Dixon, *On the Psychology of Military Incompetence* (New York: Basis Books, 1976), 13-14.

philosophy. Granted, over the years a hand full of instructors offered various useful axioms and slogans that I happily retained. These no doubt helped me through various obstacles and trials, particularly in combat. Sayings like, "Two is one, and one is none." Or "It's better to have and not need, than to need and not have." I could go on. However, in reflection, I lament the fact that none of these excellent warrior schools offered a comprehensive warrior philosophy. That is the goal of this book.

Now, let not the mere mentioning of the word "philosophy" disparage you from further reading. The discipline of philosophy, if I may be allowed to call it that, enables one to think on a level that penetrates to the deeper significance of things, helping us to organize our thoughts about the world and ourselves. In the words of philosopher Ludwig Wittgenstein, "the object of philosophy is the logical clarification of thought."

Philosophy helps us to think critically, permitting us to better arrange and systematize facts. Usually thought of being the purview of academics, philosophy is every human being's gateway to the greatest adventure of the human spirit. In fact, as I hope to show, the greatest warrior systems are undergirded by a martial philosophy. With this in mind, the principle aim of this book is to present a comprehensive system which I now refer to as *American Warrior Philosophy*.

While not all philosophies are created equal, most can be defined as having at least three component parts: (1) it views the world in a certain way, (2) it has presuppositions to support that view, and (3) it suggests principles to live by. Borne out of our distinctive traditions, founded on the truth of the Bible, and standing in defense of our Constitution, *American Warrior Philosophy* views our warrior class of Soldiers, Sailors, Airmen, and Marines as the guardians of our Republic. As such, our mission is to support and defend the Constitution of the United States against all enemies, foreign and domestic; to deploy, engage, and destroy, the enemies of the United States in close combat.

According to the historian J. Rufus Fears, a great book is one that has a great theme, that can speak across the ages, is written in noble language, and speaks to us individually. While I hope you believe what you hold in your hand is a great book, it certainly has a great theme, and that theme is: the warrior class maintains the safety, security, and survival of the State. As borne out by history, it's the doom of Nations that they forget this.

One of the saddest things I ever heard was when an old soldier lamented, "Our warrior class is dying." He's right. Weak men are a danger to the survival of America. Worthless males have been turned into "pliable material for complex manipulation." It is not tinfoil-hatted to say that America is indeed in trouble.

Where did we go wrong? Perhaps Nietzsche offers the most poignant explanation. In his work, the Gay Science, Nietzsche satirically prognosticated the death of Western civilization when he observed, "God is dead." Fair enough. We can simply dismiss God and go about our business. Not so, says Nietzsche. By saying, "God is dead," he meant that God has become dead to Western society. He wasn't saying that there is no God. He said this to remind us of something very vital to the future of our civilization. He was telling us that we share a defining set of traditional beliefs, which, at the ground floor is biblical morality.

At the time that Nietzsche was writing, Darwinism was gaining ground. Many were espousing the belief that existence is merely a random event. Nietzsche wanted us to understand that without biblical morality there is no truth. Most importantly to us, without biblical morality, our civilization will collapse. As professor Michael Sugrue has put it, without grounding our knowledge in truth, "there is simply no certain knowledge to have. All we have is an infinite number of perspectives, none of which has any ultimate grounding." Relativism, as this is called, is problematic, because "my truth" is different from "your truth." There simply cannot be a reality in such a view.

Nietzsche saw where we were headed – nihilism – values lose their values, truth is relative, there are no absolutes, and life loses its purpose, meaning and intrinsic value. Friends, I believe we are there.

But something can be done about it. "The only thing necessary for the triumph of evil is for good men to do nothing." If necessity is the mother of invention, and if the most powerful thing is an idea whose time has come, then its high time for a volume that lauds the age-old traditions and customs of the warrior class that has defended America for two and a half centuries.

As Hegel once put it, the owl of Minerva only flies after sunset. Or as we moderns put it, hindsight is twenty-twenty. The point is, there are indeed lessons of the past that endure throughout the ages. It is my heartfelt aim that Soldiers, Airmen, Sailors, and Marines benefit from my contribution. Earlier I mentioned some of the most famous statements of Clausewitz. There is one more, however overlooked, that I feel best captures the necessity of an able-bodied and virtuous warrior class. "In tactics the means are the fighting forces...the end is victory. Those are the objects which will lead directly to peace." To paraphrase, the absolute purpose of having a military is to achieve a "better state of peace." In the words of Vegetius, "*Igitur qui desiderat pacem, præparet bellum.*" Let him who desires peace prepare for war.

The Boston Massacre, March 5, 1770.

1

From Code to Virtue

"I see many soldiers; could I but see many warriors!"
– Nietzsche, *Thus Spake Zarathustra*

As theorized by Carl Gustav Jung, within mankind's collective unconscious resides the stored wisdom of accumulated ages, and thousands of generations. In this "collective unconscious," Jung identified twelve primary "archetypes" which represent the range of basic human motivations. From the grey mists of neolithic history one such archetypal motivation has been what Jung called the "hero." The subset of this archetype that resides in collective mankind, and individuals, is the "warrior." In distinction to other archetypes, the primary motivation of the "warrior" is "to leave a mark on the world."[1] Laying beneath the threshold of consciousness, this archetypal motivation dominates the personalities of those called to bear arms in defense of their kindred. Whether or not archetypes exist, it would be an unpardonable error to overlook the fact that warriors exist across all eras and nations and are in fact virtually identical in every culture. No Promethean gift here.

Nonetheless, nature abhors a vacuum. From earliest recorded history, warriors needed a code. An ethos to follow. Therefore, throughout history, the world's warrior class, be they the Roman Legionaries, the Samurai, or the Knights, all upheld behavioral codes that both fortified the character and regulated the conduct of their members. The brutalities of combat necessitated this. While such codes sought to govern violence, history's collective endowment of stories, sagas, and songs extoll the warrior virtues our forebears wished to promote.

In her excellent book, *The Code of the Warrior: Exploring Warrior Values Past and Present*, Shannon E. French explains that:

Warrior cultures throughout history and from diverse regions around the globe have constructed codes of behavior, based on that culture's image of the ideal warrior. These codes have not

---

[1] Carl G. Jung, *The Concept of the Collective Unconscious* (Princeton, NJ: Princeton University press, 1969), 43.

always been written down or literally codified into a set of explicit rules. A code can be hidden in the lines of epic poems or implied by the descriptions of mythic heroes. One way or another, it is carefully conveyed to each succeeding generation of warriors. These codes tend to be quite demanding. They are often closely linked to a culture's religious beliefs and can be connected to elaborate (and frequently death defying or excruciatingly painful) rituals and rites of passage.

In many cases this code of honor seems to hold the warrior to a higher ethical standard than that required for an ordinary citizen within the general population of the society the warrior serves. The code is not imposed from the outside. The warriors themselves police strict adherence to these standards; with violators being shamed, ostracized, or even killed by their peers. One historical example comes from the Roman legions, where if a man fell asleep while he was supposed to be on watch in time of war he could expect to be stoned to death by the members of his own cohort. The code of the warrior not only defines how he should interact with his own warrior comrades, but also how he should treat other members of his society, his enemies, and the people he conquers. The code restrains the warrior. It sets boundaries on his behavior. It distinguishes honorable acts from shameful acts.

By setting standards of behavior for themselves, accepting certain restraints, and even honoring their enemies, warriors can create a lifeline that will allow them to pull themselves out of the hell of war and reintegrate themselves into the society, should they survive to see peace restored. A warrior's code may cover everything from the treatment of prisoners of war to oath keeping to table etiquette, but its primary purpose is to grant nobility to the warrior's profession.[2]

Clearly, the greatest warriors have always held themselves to codes of honor. In the Old Testament, in what is perhaps the oldest code, God imposed limitations on the warlike activities of the Israelites. When the Israelites were conquering the Promised Land, they were commanded to slaughter all the inhabitants of the cities they captured. To show mercy was in fact a sin against Yahweh. However brutal, this was a crusade that God initiated, as Israel was under the direct rule of God (theocracy). Then, in the times of the Hebrew kings, prisoners of war were to be treated humanely. During the wars with Syria, the Prophet Elisha would not let King Jehoram slay his captured foes. Instead, the king was to "set food and water before them" (2 Kings 6:21-22).

Likewise, other ancient peoples considered it prudent to impose controls to their warlike activities. In his famous work *The Art of War*, Sun Tzu listed five character requirements for generals (leaders):[3]

1. Intelligent
2. Trustworthy
3. Humane
4. Courageous
5. Disciplined

---

[2] Shannon E. French, *The Code of the Warrior: Exploring Warrior Values Past and Present* (Lanham, MD: Rowman & Littlefield Publishers, 2016), 4.

[3] Samuel B. Griffith, *Sun Tzu: The Art of War* (London: Oxford University Press, 1963), 65.

The Five Warrior Virtues

As they say, conduct follows character. As Sun Tzu insisted, in war one should only attack the enemy combatants, arguing that "the worst policy is to attack cities." As he saw it, "there has never been a protracted war from which a country has benefited."[4] In this vein, he argued, "it is better to recapture an army entire than to destroy it, to capture a regiment, a detachment or a company entire than to destroy them." Sun Tzu's point is, "the acme of skill is to subdue your enemy without fighting."[5]

For the ancient Greeks, their law of war was primarily an unwritten set of norms arising from religious customs. Violations of these laws could result in divine punishments. Herodotus records that both Athens and Sparta suffered the gods' righteous indignation for the killing of Persian emissaries.[6] One norm was the inviolability of sacred places and observances. Temples, sanctuaries, and shrines were under divine protection and were not to be disturbed. Invaders who killed or enslaved the inhabitants of a sacked city were therefore expected to spare the religious officials.[7] Likewise, hostilities during religious festivals such as the Olympic games was considered inappropriate.

During the second Persian invasion of Greece (480 BC), Herodotus records that the Athenians called on the

[4] Ibid., 73.
[5] Ibid., 77.
[6] Herodotus, 7.133-136.
[7] Adriaan Lanni, *The Laws of War in Ancient Greece. Law and History Review*, 26(3), 469-489.

army of Sparta to help them fight the invaders. The devout Spartans explained that they could not march to war during their religious festival of Karneia, celebrated in honor of Apollo. On occasion, this norm was even manipulated to gain advantage, as when Argos changed the date of a festival in an unsuccessful attempt to forestall a Spartan attack.[8]

As far as regards actual combat, in Greece, the code of honor generally required simply "helping one's friends and hurting one's enemies." As such, observes Adriaan Lanni,

There was no convention requiring fighters to show mercy to enemy combatants defeated in battle. This was true even if they attempted to surrender. The victor had the option of killing the enemy soldiers on the spot, enslaving them, or exchanging them for ransom. All three practices are well attested in our sources. Massacres could be gruesome. The Spartans set fire to a forest where fleeing Argive fighters had taken refuge, killing thousands. In another episode the Athenians stoned to death the surviving enemy soldiers. The killing of captives on the battlefield was so well accepted that our sources generally don't bother to comment on why the victorious army chose this option. It seems likely that the choice was made based on self-interest: execution would prevent enemy soldiers in a long running conflict from fighting again, while enslavement and ransom brought financial reward.[9]

To the victor go the spoils. As an established norm, a victorious polis had complete discretion over how to treat

---

[8] Ibid.
[9] Ibid.

its vanquished enemy. Xenophon declared "there is an eternal law among all mankind, that whenever a city is taken in warfare, both the people and their possessions belong to those who captured the city." Likewise, Aristotle observed, "the law is an agreement by which they say that the things conquered in war are the property of the conqueror."

In his *History of the Peloponnesian War*, Thucydides provides an account of the debate in the Athenian Assembly over the fate of Mytilene, a neighboring polis who had surrendered after a long siege. The Athenians assembled to vote on whether to kill the entire male population. Urged on by Cleon, the Athenians voted to massacre the men of Mytilene and enslave everyone else but relented the next day and killed only the leaders of the revolt.

Various other norms had religious origins, such as the respectful treatment and return of the enemy dead. Stripping a dead soldier to claim his armor was normal, but mutilating his body was contrary to established practice. Achilles famous mutilating of Hector's body was sacrilege. Upon the end of combat, victors were required to hand over the dead to the enemy.

Thucydides recounts an occasion when this law was likewise broken. Following a battle with the Boeotians, who took up their own dead, an Athenian herald's request for the dead was refused. The Athenian herald barked that the Boeotians had "done wrong in transgressing the law of the Hellenes."

Chapter 1: From Code to Virtue

Suffice it to say, warfare in ancient Greece was brutal. In search of the traits valued in an ancient Greek warrior leads one to scour everything from Homer's *Iliad* to Plato's *Republic*. Few would argue that an allegiance to one's polis, courage, and a sense of honor would not be fair attributes lauded by Homer. Surmising that war is a necessary evil, in his *Republic*, Plato listed at least five qualities of soldiers:

1. Fierceness (spirited)
2. Physical strength
3. Honor
4. Courage
5. Competitive ambition

For Plato, soldiers are rightly honored as the guardians of the republic. As such, just taking up a shield or other weapon will not make a man capable of this task. Regarding spiritedness, Plato recognized that aggressiveness and such impulses as anger needed to be tamed and controlled by the rationally minded higher level of Guardians, the philosophic Rulers, whom the warriors would obey.[10]

Echoing the sentiment of Plato, the chief concern of the Spartans was war. The saying, "actions speak louder than words" would be an appropriate expression of their way of life. As such, a Spartan axiom is "less is more." This is all the more impressive considering that the word "Spartan" today is synonymous with simplicity and

---

[10] Plato, *The Republic*, Book II, 374.

austerity. Perhaps the best description of their character comes to us from Socrates:

They conceal their wisdom, and pretend to be blockheads, so that they may seem to be superior only because of their prowess in battle. This is how you may know that I am speaking the truth and that the Spartans are the best educated in philosophy and speaking: if you talk to any ordinary Spartan, he seems to be stupid, but eventually, like an expert marksman, he shoots in some brief remark that proves you to be only a child. [11]

In learning from these "masters of less," one of the drawbacks we have is they left little in writing. In fact, much of what we know of their culture comes to us from the writings of Plutarch, who himself was an outsider. According to him, a Spartan marching song "was such as to excite courage and boldness, and contempt for death." [12] This is a good summation.

As to Spartan warrior virtues, to Plato's list, I would add only "obedience." Illustrating this Lacedemonian virtue, as recounted by Plutarch, as a Spartan was in the thick of the fight and was about to bring down his sword on an enemy soldier, "the recall sounded, and he checked the blow. When someone inquired why, when he had his enemy in his power, he did not kill him, he said, 'Because it is better to obey one's commander than to slay an enemy.'" [13]

---

[11] Plato, *Protagoras* 342b.
[12] Plutarch, *The Ancient Customs of the Spartans.*
[13] Plutarch, *Sayings of Spartans.*

In line with the practices described in the Old Testament, a similar code applied in the Islamic world. The Caliph Abu Bakr commanded his forces "let there be no perfidy, no falsehood in your treaties with the enemy, be faithful to all things, proving yourselves upright and noble and maintaining your word and promises truly." Similarly, Islamic laws forbad the killing of women, children and the old or blind, the crippled and the helplessly insane. Moreover, prisoners of war were not to be killed, but rather ransomed, set free, or converted to Islam.

Contrary to popular belief, Vikings likewise developed warrior codes. However, theirs was hid away "in the lines of epic poems." As such, the Norse Sagas are unique historical sources about Viking warrior culture. A Saga is a story, or telling in prose, sometimes mixed with verse. In the mythical Sagas, the wondrous deeds of heroes of old time, half-gods and half-men, are told as they were handed down from father to son.[14] Among the most famous is the Volsunga Saga, which relates the tales of Sigmund and Signy, and of Sigmund's son, the hero Sigurd, the dragon slayer.[15]

As the Volsunga Saga begins, King Volsung's daughter, Signy, is to be married against her will to King Siggeir of Gotland. A feast is held in King Volsung's hall. The king's hall is built around the trunk of an ancient oak tree.

---

[14] Jesse L. Byock, *The Sagas of Volsungs* (Berkeley, CA: California Press, 1990), 37.
[15] In the German epic, *Nibelungenlied* (Song of the Nibelungs) Sigurd is called Siegfried.

Disguised as an old man, Odin, the one-eyed Norse god of war, comes to the feast and thrusts a sword in the oak to the hilt. Siggeir tries to free it but fails. Only Sigmund can free the weapon. When the King of Gotland offers to buy it, Sigmund refuses, and Siggeir flies off in anger. Siggeir invites Volsung and his sons to join him at his own hall. But they sailed into a trap. As the Saga recounts:

They set off in three ships, all well manned, and the voyage went well. When they arrived off Gotland and their ships it was already late in the evening. That same evening Signy, the daughter of king Volsung, came and called her father and brothers together for a private talk. She told them of King Siggeir's plans: that Siggeir had gathered an unbeatable army, and "he plans to betray you." "Now I ask you," she said, "to return once to your own kingdom and gather the largest force you can; then come back here and avenge yourselves. But do not put yourselves in this trap, for you will not escape his treachery if you do not do as I advise."

King Volsung then spoke: "All peoples will bear witness that I spoke one word and made the vow that fear would not make me run from neither fire nor iron. Up to this moment I've acted accordingly, and why should I not keep it in old age? Maidens will not taunt my sons during games that they feared to meet death, for every man must die sometime – there's no escape from dying the once! And my decision is that we will not run but for our own part, we will act the bravest. I have fought on a hundred occasions, sometimes I had a bigger force and sometimes it's been smaller. Both ways I have had the victory, and it will not be reported that I either fled or asked for peace.[16]

---

[16] *Volsunga Saga*, Chapter 5.

Chapter 1: From Code to Virtue

This passage underscores several key attributes valued by Northmen. King Volsung's sense of honor required of him not to flee. He could not leave merely to save his own skin. Not running from the threat also displayed his courage, and self-reliance.

The Volsunga Saga likewise demonstrates the exceeding importance of restoring honor. On their way to Siggeir's hall, King Volsung and his sons are ambushed in a forest. Volsung is killed in the fray, and his sons are taken prisoner. They are left in the forest in stocks. Each night, a she-wolf devours them, one by one. The last son, Signy's twin, Sigmund, is rescued, and remains in the woods, plotting his revenge on Siggeir.

Signy's desire for vengeance knows no bounds. She disguises herself as a gypsy, seduces her brother Sigmund, and conceives a son she names Sinfiotli. When he is a young man, Sinfiotli is sent to his uncle/father. Sigmund trains Sinfiotli as a warrior. The two of them then plot revenge but are captured and cast into Siggeir's dungeon. However, Signy is able to cast a bundle of straw into Sigmund's cell before it is locked. Hidden in the straw is Balmung, Sigmund's magic sword that he drew from the oak. Balmung's blade breaks the lock of his cell, and Sigmund and Sinfiotli spring free. Together, they kill Siggeir and his men, then set his feast hall aflame. Refusing to be saved, and desirous of restoring her family's honor, Signy tells Sigmund that Sinfiotli is his son, then consigns herself to the flames, backing into the burning palace. Evidently, Signy saw herself as the very reason for her family's dishonor.

Despite the tendency at exaggeration, as a common denominator, more important than physical deeds are the mental qualities of a Norse warrior. For the Vikings, courage in combat even in the face of death, along with a cold-heartedness against the enemy were at the center of interest. This is evidenced in the words of Sigmund's son, Sigurd, "When men meet foes in fight, better is a stout heart than a sharp sword."[17]

As is generally accepted, a representation of Norse warrior prowess is found in the poem *Havamal*. It celebrates the following virtues: [18]

1. Honor
2. Courage
3. Truth
4. Fidelity
5. Discipline
6. Hospitality
7. Industriousness
8. Self-Reliance
9. Perseverance

Here is a sampling of lines:

"Non-daring people think they will live forever if they manage to avoid strife; but old age will give no one peace, even if the spears do."[19]

---

[17] Ibid., Chapter 19.
[18]Paul Acker and Carolyne Larrington, *The Poetic Edda: Essays On Old Norse Mythology* (London: Routledge, 2016).
[19] *Havamal,* 16.

Chapter 1: From Code to Virtue

"The immoderate man, unless he watches himself closely will over-consume to his deadly sorrow. His belly makes a mockery of him, gives him away, when he tries to sit in the company of the wise."[20]

"A farm of your own is good, even if it's tiny; each man is a king in his own house. Even if you only have two goats and a roof made of ropes, that's better than having to beg for things."[21]

When out in the fields, don't go further than a footstep from your weapons; you never know for sure, out in the wild, how close a need might be for a spear."[22]

"Generous and fearless is the best way to live; people like that seldom harbor many troubles. But the non-daring are afraid of everything, and misers are always upset over having to give."[23]

"One fire takes its power from another, till it is consumed. One spark only springs from another spark. A man becomes wise and witty by talking with others, but fools remain foolish by remaining isolated."[24]

"He will rise early, he who wants to take from another person their wealth or their life. Seldom does a

---

[20] Ibid., 20.
[21] Ibid., 36.
[22] Ibid., 38.
[23] Ibid., 48.
[24] Ibid., 57.

slumbering wolf get a ham, nor a sleeping man a victory."[25]

"A lame man can still ride a horse. A man without hands can still herd beasts. A deaf man can be daring in battle."[26]

"Two are as dangerous as an army against a lone man. The tongue is the greatest danger to the head. Under each fur-cloak, I expect to see a fist."[27]

"Praise the day at evening, a woman on her pyre, a weapon after it's tried, a maiden at her wedding, ice after it's crossed, ale after it's drunk."[28]

"Cattle die, and kinsmen die, and we will die ourselves; but fair fame never dies for the one who can achieve it."[29]

At the ground floor of our Western tradition lies the notion of chivalry. Despite the modern tendency to devalue everything, chivalry was a highly serious code by which men-at-arms lived and died by standards of courtesy, fair play, and respect for God, Country, and women. An in-depth view of the medieval chivalric world is handed down to us by the French knight Geoffrey de Charny (1300-1356).

---

[25] Ibid., 58.
[26] Ibid., 71.
[27] Ibid., 73.
[28] Ibid., 81.
[29] Ibid., 176.

Chapter 1: From Code to Virtue

Charny's career was shaped by the Anglo-French conflict known as the Hundred Years War (1337–1453), in which France faced near extinction. In the history of nations, at every point of crisis, of crucial importance, is the recovery of the high ideals of the warrior class. Following the disastrous Battle of Crecy in 1346, which cut down the flower of French chivalry, Charny was commissioned by French King Jean II to compose a series of works that would invigorate French élan (vigorous spirit), inspiring knights to live up to chivalric standards. Of the many qualities lauded by Charny, among the most chivalric is fealty (loyalty) to own's feudal lord.

In his book, *A Knight's Own Book of Chivalry*, Geoffrey de Charny describes the way of the knight, along with its requisite virtues. Writing in an age of edged weaponry, at a time of routine military violence which resulted in massive civilian casualties, chivalry was an effort to set ground rules for knightly behavior. This reminds us of two important truths. First, the military profession involves the management of violence, and second, the warrior culture is separate from society albeit subservient to it.

As a martial philosopher, Charny was a man who could artfully and poignantly systematize his thoughts about his chosen profession, as well as a man who could organize and lead a blood-curdling cavalry charge. Regarding loyalty, Charny observed that a worthy knight is one who swears fealty to the king as well as to the order to which he belongs and wages war:

In the defense of the honor and inheritance of their kinsmen, or like those who stay to serve in the wars to defend the honor and inheritance of their rightful lord who maintains them, for the faith and loyalty which they owe to their lord cannot be better demonstrated than by serving him and assisting him loyally in such urgent need as that of war which is so grave as to put person, land and resources all at risk.[30]

Living up to the standards of the order he inspired, Charny carried the French royal standard into battle, and was hacked to death at the Battle of Poitiers defending his sovereign, King Jean II. As it is related, before he was killed, Charny cut down the first man to lay a hand on the bridle of King Jean's horse. Hailed as a "true and perfect knight" by his contemporaries, Charny's book achieved its aim, revitalizing the knight's code, proving that chivalry was not dead. It still isn't. Works like that of Charny's also remind us that the greatest warrior systems are undergirded by a martial philosophy.

The quality of chivalry reminds us that combat is ceremonial. That is, combat is a formal event that is regulated by a system of rules. Opponents are to be respectful, showing honor to each other as members of the fraternity of arms. The following oath is found on the tombstone of a knight in Malta:

I do solemnly swear by Almighty God and His Name, and in free and voluntary desire, to serve as a Knight of Malta of the most holy Order of Saint John of Jerusalem. I do swear by the

---

[30] Richard W. Kaeuper and Elspeth Kennedy, *The Book of Chivalry of Geoffroi de Charny: Text, Context, and Translation* (The Middle Ages Series) (Philadelphia: University of Pennsylvania Press, 1996), 49.

Chapter 1: From Code to Virtue

Eternal Power of the Trinity, to be both a true and chivalric Knight, to obey my Commanders and to aid my brethren. I also swear by all that is holy and dear unto me, to aid those less fortunate than I, to relieve the distress of the world and to fulfill my knightly obligations. This oath do I give of my own free and independent will, so help me God! Amen!

The ideals of Knighthood, and their code of chivalry are found in the many poems and literary works of medieval authors. Like all other codes, chivalry came into existence because it was needed to give knights a code of conduct. In the words of French military historian Leon Gautier, "Chivalry is the Christian form of the military profession: the knight is the Christian soldier."[31] As such, chivalry may be considered an eighth sacrament. As argued by Gautier, there are six virtues of chivalry: [32]

1. Honor
2. Forbearance (Self-Control)
3. Hardihood
4. Largesse (Generosity)
5. Benevolence
6. Loyalty

Similar in form and content to its European cousin, Japanese Bushido likewise took centuries to articulate. Bushido is the code of conduct of Japan's warrior class. The word "bushido" comes from the Japanese root words "bushi" meaning "warrior," and "do" meaning "way." The absolute quintessence of the samurai ideal was to be immune from the fear of death. Only the fear of dishonor

---

[31] Leon Gautier, *Chivalry* (London: George Routledge and Sons, 1891), 2.
[32] Ibid.

motivated the true samurai. While European chivalry forbade suicide, in Bushido it was the ultimate act of bravery.

According to Bushido, a samurai who lost his honor could regain it by committing an act of ritualistic suicide called "seppuku." By committing seppuku, a samurai would not only regain his honor, he would also gain prestige for facing death with equanimity. Bushido translates to "way of the warrior." Arguably, it has been best articulated by Inazo Nitobe. In his book, *Bushido, The Soul of Japan*, Nitobe enumerates eight virtues:[33]

1. Honor
2. Courage
3. Benevolence
4. Politeness
5. Honesty
6. Justice
7. Loyalty
8. Self-control

I have more to say about Bushido in chapters three and six. In passing, suffice to say that like chivalry, Bushido went beyond the battlefield so as to encompass every aspect of a warrior's existence.

In my chronology, I purposely skipped over the Romans until now. Writing during a period of Rome's decline, Publius Vegetius Renatus, known as Vegetius, sought to reinvigorate the fighting spirit of the Eternal City. In his work, *De re militari*, Latin for *Concerning*

---

[33] Inazo Nitobe, *Bushido: The Sword of Japan* (Rutland, VT: Tuttle, 1969).

Military Matters, Vegetius provides much by way of what it was like to be a Roman soldier in the 4th Century. In the Roman manner of assimilation, he lauds the same virtues as that of ancient Greece. What is different, and highly thought provoking, is his arguments that he makes regarding the absolute imperative of maintaining a strong warrior class. For Vegetius, it is the warrior class that maintains the safety, security, and survival of the State.

Watching Rome deteriorate around him he observed that, "The decline and eventual fall of Rome was due primarily to the warrior class straying away from their ideals." As he argued, in reviving the warrior class, Rome's greatness could be revived as well. Putting his hand on a live nerve, Vegetius lamented how peace can create complacency:

A sense of security born of long peace has diverted mankind partly to the enjoyment of private leisure, partly to civilian careers. Thus, attention to military training obviously was at first discharged rather neglectfully, then omitted, until finally consigned long since to oblivion.[34]

Further, as Vegetius argued, quality trumps quantity. As such he stated, "In every battle it is not numbers and untaught bravery so much as skill and training that generally produce the victory." Further, in his opinion, the rural populace was better suited to the profession of arms. The reason for this is that those from the country "are nurtured under the open sky in a life of work,

---

[34] Vegetius, *De re militari.*

enduring the sun, careless of shade, are unacquainted with bathhouses, and ignorant of luxury."

Moreover, they are "simple-souled, content with a little, with limbs toughened to endure every kind of toil, and for whom wielding iron, digging a fosse (trench line) and carrying a burden is what they are used to." However, as he admits, at times "necessity demands that city-dwellers also be conscripted."[35]

No doubt, Vegetius meant that urban men had to develop a taste for hardship before they could be taught to be warriors. He goes on to say:

They must work, drill, carry a burden and endure heat and dust; they must adopt a moderate, rural diet, and camp under the sky, under tents. Only then should they be trained in the use of arms and, if a long campaign is in prospect, they should be detained for considerable period on outpost-duty and be kept far away from the attractions of the city, so that by this means their physical and mental vigor may be increased.[36]

Reaching back to the glory that was Rome's, Vegetius sought to recover the martial spirit that had once conquered the known world. As he argued:

These skills were formerly maintained in use, as well as in books, but once they were abandoned it was a long time before anyone needed them, because with the flourishing of peacetime pursuits the imperatives of war were far removed. But lest it be thought impossible for an art to be revived whose use has been lost, let us be instructed by precedents. Among

---

[35] Ibid., Book III, 89.
[36] Ibid., Book I, 4.

the ancients, military science often fell into oblivion, but at first it was recovered from books, and later consolidated by the authority of generals. Scipio Africanus took over our armies in Spain after they had been several times beaten under other commanders. By observing the rules of discipline, he trained these so thoroughly in every article of work and digging of fosses, that he said that they deserved to be stained by digging mud, because they had declined to be wetted by the enemy's blood.[37]

Perhaps Vegetius' entire argument through a twenty-first century lens could be surmised as follows: "Hard times create strong men, strong men create good times, good times create weak men, and weak men create hard times." These lessons offered by Vegetius are indeed lessons of the past that endure throughout the ages. As I will argue, we likewise neglect these lessons to our doom.

In this same stream of conscious thought, in his great treatise *On War*, Carl von Clausewitz echoes the argument of Vegetius by saying that "the moral elements in war are among the most important."[38] Warriors are not mere hired killers. As such, he went on to argue that a warrior code restrains a warrior. And that, "The soldiers trade, if it is to mean anything at all, has to be anchored to an unshakeable code of honor. Otherwise, those of us who follow the drums become nothing more than a bunch of hired assassins walking around in gaudy clothes... a disgrace to God and mankind."

---

37 Ibid., Book III, 89.
38 Clausewitz, *On War*, Book III, Chapter 3, 216-220.

The Five Warrior Virtues

As it may be deduced from his seminal work *On War*, Clausewitz enumerates at least nine military virtues:

1. Bravery
2. Obedience
3. Professional pride (esprit de corps)
4. Adaptability
5. Stamina
6. Enthusiasm (military spirit)
7. Honor
8. Boldness (governed by intellect)
9. Perseverance

Demonstrating how the moral elements in war are among the most important, Clausewitz summed up his concern for the maintenance of such warrior virtues by declaring:

If there is a lesson to be drawn from these facts, it is that when an army lacks military virtues, every effort should be made to keep operations as simple as possible. The mere fact that soldiers belong to a 'regular army' does not automatically mean they are equal to their tasks.[39]

In other words, cutting the muster to serve in the armed forces doesn't necessarily constitute one has the necessary moral fiber of being a good serviceman. For as he suggests, lengthy operations will expose immoral men as who they are. So true! The mission of the warrior class is to execute the foreign policy objectives of the United States; to deploy, engage, and destroy, our enemies in close combat. That is not the only mission of the military,

---

[39] Ibid., 221.

but it is the principal one. And as I would argue, simply being a part of the armed forces does not necessarily mean one has the necessary virtues required to serve with honor.

Echoing Vegetius' sentiment, warriors are the guardians of our Republic. The absolute raison d'etre of the American warrior class is to defend the Nation, and the State, even when it's not appreciated. Works from those like Vegetius remind us that in every age, the vicissitude of societal change necessitates a demand for the warrior class to return to first principles in order to maintain focus, vitality, and lethality.

I began by listing several Army courses I was privileged to attend. Now that I'm twenty years removed from such lessons as these schools provide, I lament that none of them offered a philosophy. To be sure, volumes of warrior materiel was recommended. Books like, T. E. Lawrence's *Seven Pillars of Wisdom,* James Nick Rowe's *Five Years to Freedom,* and Franklin D. Miller's *Reflections of a Warrior* to name a few. Such works are justifiably widely read, and no doubt showcase warrior deeds. Few however, as I have discovered, are about warrior virtues.

There are also many great works on soldiering and tactics. For example, most service academy reading lists include such seminal volumes as, Sun Tzu *The Art of War*, Carl von Clausewitz *On War*, and Antoine Jomini *The Art of War*. While these volumes are invaluable, laying out the foundational tenets of the art and science of war, with some exception, much like the above-mentioned works, they lack a systematic arrangement of the warrior virtues they extoll. Last, but not least, is the *Army Values* and the *Warrior Ethos*. Adopted in 1995, these articulations define the desired character of all soldiers, and acts as a guide to action on and off duty. There are seven Army values: **LDRSHIP**

Loyalty
Duty
Respect
Selfless Service
Integrity
Honor
Personal Courage

Consider the words of the *Warrior Ethos*:

I will always place the mission first.
I will never accept defeat.
I will never quit.
I will never leave a fallen comrade.

According to FM 3-21.75, *The Warrior Ethos and Soldier Combat Skills*, "the warrior culture is a shared set of important beliefs, values, and assumptions. It is crucial and perishable. Its martial ethic connects American warriors of today with those whose previous sacrifices allowed our nation to persevere. You, the individual Soldier, are the foundation for the warrior culture. As in larger institutions, the Armed Forces' use culture, in this case warrior culture, to let people know they are part of something bigger than just themselves; they have responsibilities not only to the people around them, but also to those who have gone before and to those who will come after them. The warrior culture is a part of who you are, and a custom you can take pride in."[40]

The above quote is a great starting point. Albeit, in my thinking, while such articulations are fine and good in their own way, all this material we've surveyed in this chapter offers little more than a "chaos of arbitrary opinions." Despite the many volumes pertaining to the worthy subject of American warrior culture, it remains, nonetheless, an unexplored field of study. It is hoped that this volume fills the perceived void.

This book seeks to define and extoll, that is, call to embody, five warrior virtues. What is a virtue? The answer to that question is what this book is all about. At the most basic level, according to Aristotle, virtue is a state of character, the sum of individual qualities. In ancient Greek, the word for "virtue" is *arete* meaning "praiseworthy excellence." My intent is to survey five warrior virtues, which as I will argue, are the five virtues of the ideal warrior. The five warrior virtues that are presented in this book are consistent with the world's warrior codes. These virtues are:

1. Honor
2. Integrity
3. Loyalty
4. Temperance
5. Courage

---

[40] FM 3-21.75, *The Warrior Ethos and Soldier Combat Skills.*

The Five Warrior Virtues

Can warriors still get the job done if they do not have a code or live according to virtues? Yes, but invariably they'll be nothing more than highly trained immoral men. Men that others would no doubt not want to serve with, and who, in the course of time, will fail no doubt because they lack honor, integrity, or some other virtue. It goes without saying that such virtues have been taken for granted. A dangerous practice indeed is assuming that everyone knows and lives these virtues out. To do so is unsound.

My aim is to argue that these virtues are in fact imperatives. They are "musts" for a warrior to serve with honor. For many serve but not all serve with honor. As I will argue, as these virtues are sought after and lived, they will bring honor to the warrior who practices them. Not only that, but these qualities are also demanded by fellow warriors. Why these five and not others? Excellent question. In an independent survey, which took over a year, and involved the feedback from nearly every branch of service, the following was discovered:

1. Are there such things as warrior virtues? 100% said yes.

2. If so, how many are there? Most answered between four and five, with honor heading the list, following by integrity, discipline, and courage.

3. Why are warrior virtues important? The standard answer was that they form the very foundation of the warrior culture.

4. Can a man serve with distinction without these virtues? 100% said no.

5. When it comes to the virtues you listed, where do you feel we are at on a national level? Invariably, this question was answered as, "not very well." Those surveyed cited moral decay as the culprit, noting that, only those who choose to serve have these virtues. Tellingly, as one observed, "if we lack the courage to pass these virtues on to the next generation of warriors, we will doom America's future to the dust bin of history." I couldn't agree more.

In light of the surveyed warrior codes, one of my difficulties was arriving at a finite number of virtues. The possibilities seem endless. Particularly difficult was the question of how many are in our own American warrior tradition. This presupposes that we have our own distinctive American version of warrior virtues. This question remains to be answered. However, like other nations, the warrior virtues that have been placed on a high premium have not always been written down or literally codified, but rather, they have likewise been hidden away in stories and songs or implied by the descriptions of our heroes.

Moreover, as I have sought to demonstrate, these five virtues of *honor, integrity, loyalty, temperance,* and *courage* form the foundation of every warrior code, in every nation, of every age. It is my hope that a sincere focus on these virtues will foster an environment that produces able-bodied men of fine character that will make excellent citizen-warriors. Any discussion of these virtues will therefore be either recovery or discovery. Both are good.

Beginning from the highest vantage point possible, the ground floor of *American Warrior Philosophy* is a commitment to serve the Nation – duty. A warrior is a servant of the State, a guardian of the Republic. The warrior class not only comes from society, but its ranks also hold society together. Before the age of nations, warriors banded themselves together to defend their *polis*, clan, or kindred. In every age, duty has therefore been the galvanizing spirit of all true warriors.

Chapter 1: From Code to Virtue

Famously, General Douglas MacArthur's speech to West Point extolled the virtues of duty, honor, and Country. Duty is also encapsulated in the third stanza of the Ranger Creed: "Never shall I fail my comrades. I will always keep myself mentally alert, physically strong, and morally straight and I will shoulder more than my share of the task whatever it may be, one hundred percent and then some." For the American warrior, duty is therefore the privilege of service. It is a warrior's commitment to serve the Nation.

As I have attempted to show, warriors of every generation sensed the urgency to codify what they held to be the meaningful truths of what it means to be a warrior. As guardians of our Republic, and as our Nation drifts further into unchartered waters, the degradation of society warrants we do the same. It is therefore all the more important for those of us who defend our way of life to return to first principles. Every generation of warriors needs to be reminded of these virtues. It goes without saying then, that focusing on these basic tenets of what it means to serve the Nation in arms, reestablishes a baseline of excellence.

In America, at an alarming rate, various motivations are at play in an attempt at redefining the meaningful truths. Virtually nothing is off the table. Societal trends demonstrate the attempt at recreating other realities. If you're like me, you believe such attempts are annoying at best, dangerous at worst. As I will argue, truth is objective. It stands above us. Truth is reality. In fact, that is actually the meaning of the word. Coming to us from the Greek, the word *alétheia* (truth) means "reality," and literally means "not concealed." The point is there's only one version of the truth.

That the Founding Fathers likewise believed this is evidenced by their appeal to objective truth in the Charters of Freedom: the Declaration of Independence, the Constitution, and the Bill of Rights. When it comes to articulating the virtues of the American warrior, we need look no further than the Founding Fathers, who left us their own words on the matter. My intent is to demonstrate that these five virtues were central to men like George Washington, Thomas Jefferson, and Theodore Roosevelt. While they may not have formulated them together as five virtues, they nonetheless extoll them frequently in their writings.

Lastly, as Steven Pressfield reminds us, "No one is born with the warrior ethos, though many of its tenets appear naturally in those of all cultures. The warrior ethos is taught." This is no doubt true as centuries of warriors have passed down codes and virtues from warrior to warrior. Anything worth knowing can and should be taught. This book is an attempt toward an actionable philosophy for the American warrior. Full disclosure, I have not arrived. Every day I work at living out these virtues, to be a man of honor.

Introspection

I have purposely bookended each chapter with five introspective questions. These are designed to promote professional growth:

1. Are there such things as warrior virtues?

2. How many are there?

3. Can a warrior serve with distinction without such virtues?

4. What warrior code do you live by?

5. When it comes to warrior virtues, where do you think we are on a national level?

The Battles of Lexington and Concord, April 19, 1775.

2

Honor

"And how can man die better than facing fearful odds, for the ashes of his fathers, and the temples of his gods." – Macaulay

Honor is the foundational virtue for nearly every human endeavor. For no other profession, than the profession of arms, is this true. In Napoleon's estimation, honor is more important than life. As such, in his military maxims he remarked, "In giving battle a general should regard it as his first duty to maintain the honor and glory of his arms. To spare his troops should be but a secondary

46

consideration."[1] The Vikings agreed, saying, "Better to die with honor than live with shame."[2] However extreme, the emperor's point is, honor is more important than life. The warriors of history agree. In fact, "wherever there is even the feeblest spark of what men call duty, there is always found that mysterious and exalted feeling called honor, with whose bitter sweetness nothing else that is human is comparable, since by comparison with it life itself has a feather's weight of value."[3]

Virtue means praiseworthy excellence. Here's the ground floor of all the warrior virtues, the praiseworthy excellence of that mysterious and exalted feeling – honor. At the simplest level, honor is the status or reputation of a man in the eyes of others. Likewise, the profession of arms exists to defend honor. According to the Samurai, honor is a vivid sense of personal dignity and worth. As touching on psychology, according to Bushido, honor is a sense of calm trust in Fate, a quiet submission to the inevitable. As we go on to discuss each warrior virtue, I want to employ the triad of definition-concept-principle.

Definition

Socrates once remarked, "Wisdom begins with the definition of terms." As a definition, it may be said that honor is the one word which encapsulates the very essence of the warrior ethos (which itself is the warrior "way"). As a second Greek term, the word for honor in the

---

[1] Maxim 15.
[2] *Jomsvíkinga Saga*, Chapter 23.
[3] Baron Hugo von Freytag-Loringhoven, *The Power of Personality in War* (Harrisburg, PA: Military Service Publishing, 1955), 164.

Greek language is *timeh,* meaning "worth and value." According to the ancient Greeks, honor is a valuation of worth. Hence the expression for something lacking honor, "there's no honor in it." No discussion of honor would be complete without the mentioning of shame. Norman Dixon aptly states,

A code of honor is a set of rules for behavior. The rules are observed because to break them provokes the distressing emotions of guilt or shame. Whereas guilt is a product of knowing that one has transgressed and therefore might be found out, shame results from actually being found out – in military circles traditionally the greater crime![4]

This reminds us that, in warrior cultures, shame not only acts as a counter to fear, but it also serves as a goad to honor.

The Law of Honor

The story of America is the story of strength and honor. In the Spring of 1776, delegates from the Thirteen American Colonies met to discuss the great question of independence from Britain. With blood on the ground at Lexington, they argued that these American Colonies should be free and independent States as part of a free and sovereign Nation. "The sun never shined on a cause of greater worth." With moral courage, they drafted a statement that would declare to the world why these United States were declaring their independence from Britain. By such a declaration, we became the only nation

---

[4] Norman F. Dixon, *On the Psychology of Military Incompetence* (New York: Basis Books, 1976), 210.

in history to be founded upon moral principles claiming to the entire world that "all men are created equal, that they are endowed by their Creator with certain unalienable Rights, that among these are Life, Liberty and the pursuit of Happiness."

Having no illusions as to what they were risking, these men who signed the Declaration finished this great charter of freedom with these words, "With a firm Reliance on the Protection of divine Providence, we mutually pledge to each other our Lives, our Fortunes, and our sacred Honor."

These words, "sacred honor," encapsulate the spirit that has animated the noble words and deeds of American warriors for the past 246 years. These words, "sacred honor" once served as a barometer of both the virtue and vitality of our nation and the warrior class that defends her. It goes without saying that honor is foundational to healthy human relationships. It's vital for the maintenance of order in a civil society. Moreover, honor was, at one time, easily recognized and easily defined. But alas, we rarely hear the word honor today. And yet, the one true and enduring law for warriors throughout the ages is the law of honor.

Earlier, I mentioned MacArthur's speech to West Point where he extolled the virtues of Duty, Honor, Country. In his speech, MacArthur rightly used the word honor as a noun and a verb. As a verb, honor involves treating others with dignity and respect. As a noun, it involves adherence to doing what is right and just. As a noun, honor is a quality we ascribe to things, and as a verb, honor is like currency. It is exchanged. It redeems. Honor is adherence to duty. Honor also pertains to a warrior's worth and reputation. As such, honor can be tarnished, stained, and wounded.

It was the calling into question of his honor that led Admiral Michael Boorda to take his own life. Michael Boorda was the Chief of Naval Operations. He was a warrior for forty-years. There were questions raised by news organizations regarding his wearing of two combat pins on his Vietnam-era ribbon decorations. Allegations were made against him that he was not authorized to wear these combat pins. The controversy grew to such an extent that Boorda decided to take the drastic step of firing a bullet in his chest, in fact, right where he wore those ribbons.

As I see him, Michael Boorda was a very honorable man, who made the terrible mistake of taking his own life. I raise the memory of Admiral Boorda here, not to libel or defame him in any way, but to merely point out that the admiral was acting in a noble, if not misguided, attempt to protect the honor of the Navy. For him, honor was a sacred prize. This tragic example reminds us that honor is a high value we ascribe to things, and in many ways, the profession of arms exists to defend honor. Warriors have always believed that. That in fact was what led me to join the Army.

As the "philosopher" Jack Reacher once observed, people join the military for essentially four reasons:

Chapter 2: Honor

They're patriots looking to serve, it's a family business, they just need a job, or they're looking for a legal means of killing others. Honestly, I think I might have joined for all these reasons. My father was Navy. My grandfather was Navy. My uncles were Navy. You could say the Navy is our family business. Naturally, my father wanted me to follow his footsteps but, when I was sixteen years-old on a dependence cruise, I discovered I would never find my sea legs. And so, the Army would be the life for me.

After I enlisted, I spent the better part of eighteen months in the big Army before I got tired of seeing people okay with mediocrity, and low standards. Now, at the time, I didn't know what a warrior ethos was, (or even how to spell ethos), all I knew was I wanted to serve in a unit that placed a high premium on excellence. I wanted to serve with meat eaters. Being in the Army, I naturally gravitated toward the Special Forces. I sought the warrior way of life and a challenge. I found both in the brotherhood of the Green Berets. After another five or so years, I sensed an irresistible pull to an even higher level of the warrior way of life, with more challenges. I found that in the Unit, also known as CAG. Having successfully completed the long walk, and the Operator Training Course, I was privileged to go on and serve in the storied C Squadron.

On one of the first raids I was on with C Squadron, we hit a compound in Baquba, Iraq. We were going after two bomb makers who had been rather successful in making the roadside bombs that were taking a high toll on the lives of the 101st Airborne Division. It was 2006, the hay day of Iraq hundred-day rotations in which the Unit concentrated on decapitation strikes to destroy Al-Qaeda in Iraq (AQI).

Being a Squadron hit, our Squadron Sergeant Major "Bill" accompanied us. It was a standard raid. We arrived the target building by six-wheeled commando vehicles, then fanned out to our perspective Team breach points. Following the familiar countdown, we made entry, and rapidly cleared the objective. Nothing out of the ordinary. However, what I witnessed from Bill was extra ordinary. In one of the larger rooms, we encountered a family, and an older woman. She was about seventy something. After blowing the doors off the hinges, and violently flooding the building with assaulters, we took control of the fighting age males, and then with a gentlemen-like quality one would expect in a ballroom, Bill took the old woman by the hand and led her to an adjoining room, where he offered her a couch to sit down.

What I learned, or relearned is what medieval knights called chivalry, a quality that may be understood as the coalescence of gentleness and strength. Chivalry is essentially gentlemanly interaction with one's fellow man, be this a military opponent or a lady. As such, this quality enables a warrior to cleave a man's head in two in one room, and then gently carry an infant like a carton of eggs in the next.

Of the many aspects to chivalry perhaps the solemn rite of handling arms is the first. In his composition regarding the lives of barbarians outside the Roman Empire, Roman historian Tacitus describes this German rite.

> Without being armed they transact nothing, whether of public or private concernment. But it is repugnant to their custom for any man to use arms, before the community has attested his capacity to wield them. Upon such testimony, either one of the rulers, or his father, or some kinsman dignify the young man in the midst of the assembly, with a shield and javelin. This amongst them is the manly robe, this first degree of honor conferred upon their youth. Before this they seem no more than part of a private family, but thenceforward part of the Commonwealth.[5]

As this ancient German rite attests, it's an honor to bear arms, and the first rite of necessity to join the warrior ranks. As war is ceremonial, there are special rites to joining the brotherhood of arms. And the law of honor determines how arms are to be used. In one sense, chivalry is essentially a synonym for honor. And the one true and enduring law for warriors throughout the ages is the law of honor. In other words, honor stands above us. It has power over us. Allow me to explain.

According to the Stoic philosopher Cicero, "the law is not made, it's found." And what he meant was, the laws developed by society are an outgrowth of the natural law of right reason. Considering how honor is a law unto itself, when an action is done dishonorably, the perpetrator is villainized. Spartan women appealed to the law of honor when they intoned the immortal words,

---

[5] J. Anderson, *Germania* (Oxford: Clarendon Press, 1938).

"come home with your shield or on it." Honor transcends time and culture.

Standing above warriors, the law of honor dictates how actions are to be done. Since July 4, 1776, America has been at war 229 out of 246 years. Statistically, America has been at war 93% of the time, and at peace for less than 20 years total since its inception. America's wars span a period of over four centuries, ranging from the era of European colonization to America's interventions in Syria and Libya at the present. In hundreds of campaigns, on hundreds of battlefields, around a thousand campfires, America's prosecution of these wars has been guided by the Judeo-Christian ethic found in the Bible, which forms the ground floor of the Law of Armed Conflict (LOAC).

In this age of wokeness, this strikes many as odd, but it's simply the truth. Far from a drawn-out argument, let it be said that America was founded on Christian principles and values. In his commentary on the US Constitution, Chief Justice Joseph Story once wrote, "Every colony, from its foundation down to the revolution, with the exception of Rhode Island, (if, indeed, that state be an exception,) did openly, by the whole course of its laws and institutions, support and sustain, in some form, the Christian religion; and almost invariably gave a peculiar sanction to some of its fundamental doctrines."[6]

---

[6] Joseph Story, *Commentaries on the Constitution, Document 69*, 1867.

As the Law of Armed Conflict (LOAC) is the baseline for honorable American warfare, a brief discussion will prove beneficial. LOAC has four basic principles: (1) Military necessity, (2) distinction, (3) proportionality, and (4) unnecessary suffering. Military necessity justifies certain actions necessary to defeat an enemy and has three elements: Force necessary to secure the complete submission of the enemy as soon as possible. Force cannot be otherwise forbidden by international law. This requires that potential targets must be a legitimate military objective.[7] The principle of discrimination requires that all attacks be directed at only combatants and military targets. War is a violent contest and can be extremely destructive. The principle of proportionality therefore restricts the amount of collateral damage so that it is not excessive compared to the direct military advantage anticipated.

Writing on just war, the medieval philosopher Thomas Aquinas opined that when you have stopped the evil to go any further than that and gain an unfair advantage over the enemy, to take more of their land, take more of their money, to punish them in greater excess than what is equitable and just; then you have stopped being the prosecutors of a just war. Lastly, the principle of unnecessary suffering aims to limit warfare to prevent superfluous injury and undue suffering. These principles have been codified from earlier works. In the more recent past is the so-called Lieber Code, drafted by Professor

---

[7] A valid military objective is defined as objects, which by their nature, location, purpose, or use make an effective contribution to military action.

Francis Lieber and later promulgated as General Orders No. 100 of the Union Army in 1863.

As Sherman once so aptly stated, war is hell. As such, it's one of the most dreadful evils that can be inflicted on a people. But at times, war is inevitable and must be waged to defend its citizens and property. As Clausewitz has rightly observed, the purpose for war is to achieve a better state of the peace.

The US Congress has declared war eleven times. America's first declaration of war of June 13, 1812, stated that in response to the injustices of the British Government upon the American people, it has become necessary,

to avenge the wrongs, and vindicate the rights and honor of the nation... Your committee believing that the freeborn sons of America are worthy to enjoy the liberty which their fathers purchased at the price of so much blood and treasure, and seeing in the measures adopted by Great Britain a course commenced and persisted in which must lead to a loss of national character and independence, feel no hesitation in advising resistance by force, in which the Americans of the present day will prove to the enemy and to the world, that we have not only inherited that liberty which our fathers gave us, but also the will and power to maintain it. Relying on the patriotism of the nation, and confidently trusting that the Lord of Hosts will go with us to battle in a righteous cause, and crown our efforts with success, your committee recommend an immediate appeal to arm.

If only the US Congress spoke in such ways today? The point being, as understood by the US Congress of 1812, government bears the sword and has a right to use it at its discretion to defend itself from what it perceives to be dangerous and destructive behavior on the part of those within or without the nation state. My point is, at the foundational level of the American way of war is the Bible which makes a fundamental distinction between killing and murder. The sixth commandment (Ex 20:13) plainly states: "You shall not murder." The Hebrew word for murder *ratzach* is used forty-nine times in the Old Testament but never of war. The point is, killing and murder are not the same. Murder is illegal killing.[8]

Though clear in the Bible, there yet persists a root fallacy that killing in war is in direct opposition to the teachings of Christ and the Christian faith. Echoing this false notion, psychologist Norman Dixon writes,

The knowledge that one is a Christian, and therefore bound to the injunction 'thou shalt not kill,' and the knowledge that one is a member of a group that is even more forcibly bound to the injunction 'thou shalt kill' or, to say the least, dissonant cognitions, and therefore productive of stress. For every conscientious objector there must be many whose participation in lethal activities cannot be quite so wholehearted as some would wish.[9]

However brilliant, and correct on many other matters, here, it must be said, the doctor errs. The King James Version of Exodus 20:13, quoted by Norman Dixon,

---

[8] The King James Version which has "thou shalt not kill" is too broad. The New King James corrects this. The word is rendered "murder."
[9] Norman F. Dixon, *On the Psychology of Military Incompetence* (New York: Basis Books, 1976), 212.

which has "thou shalt not kill" is too broad. The Hebrew language has eight different words for killing, and the one used in that verse has been chosen carefully. The New King James Version of Exodus 20:13 renders it more correctly, "You shall not murder." The simple point is, the Bible makes a distinction between "murder," the illegitimate taking of life, and "killing," the legitimate taking of life. Certainly, life can be taken unlawfully. People can do evil and murder others, taking life unlawfully, and illegitimately. But killing and murder are not synonymous. The legitimate taking of life in war is killing.

As a famous example, it was once said of David that "Saul had killed his thousands but David his tens of thousands" (1 Samuel 18:7). As a young warrior, David lawfully and honorably killed thousands of the enemies of Israel. Earlier, as a young lad, he defended the honor of God. When no one else would face the Philistine champion, David slung a stone into the giant's forehead, killed him where he stood, and beheaded Goliath with his own sword (1 Samuel 17:40-51). Doing so, David became a national hero, but not out of a desire for personal glory but a love for God and a desire to bring honor to His name. David killed the enemy of his country, not out of personal vengeance, but as a lesser magistrate, and extension of the state.

Sometime later, after God had removed Saul from being king, David reigned over Israel and God's people prospered. As David grew older, he remained in his capital at Jerusalem while his army fought. One evening, as he walked on the roof of his palace, he saw Bathsheba bathing, and though she was the wife of one of his mighty men, Uriah, he slept with her and got her pregnant. Then in his attempt to cover it up, he conspired with his general, Joab, busy besieging the city of Ammon, to have Uriah killed.

In a message to Joab, David wrote, "Set Uriah in the forefront of the hottest battle, and retreat from him, that he may be struck down and die" (2 Samuel 11:16). And so, the hapless Uriah fell in battle. Afterward, when David received news of Uriah's death, he brought Bathsheba into his house, made her his wife, and she bore a son. The plot had worked – or so it seemed. "But the thing that David had done displeased the LORD" (2 Samuel 11:27). God then sent his prophet Nathan to David, who confronted him about his adultery, betrayal, and murder. As a consequence for his sin, the child died.

The point is, David was a mighty man of valor. He killed the enemies of his country, by the delegated power of the sword, but he murdered Uriah, and used the sword as a means for personal enrichment. In so doing, David desecrated the law of honor. However evil his actions, David confessed and repented, then went on to be an even greater king, demonstrating he was indeed a man after God's own heart.

The law of honor necessitates that warriors, operating under the authority of the state, which has been ordained by God, are mindful they are an extension of the state, and as such, should operate as representatives of the government and not as private citizens (Romans 13). With this mindset, American warriors thereby discharge their duties rightly and justly, including the killing of enemy combatants in war.

As the Bible teaches, it is not unlawful to kill enemies in war, provided that the war is just. Americans have long believed that a war is just only if it is waged by a legitimate government; for a worthy cause; with force proportional to the attack; against men who are soldiers not civilians; and when all other means of resolution have failed. The issue is not whether war is evil but rather is war necessary at times. The goal in a just war is to secure a condition of peace that is either being threatened or has been lost. That's why the manner it is to be waged is so important. And so, the one true and enduring law for all warriors of all time is the law of honor.

Understanding this is no light matter. As Shannon French ably comments,

To say the least, the things that warriors are asked to do to guarantee their cultures' survival are far beyond pleasant. In a sense, the nature of a warrior's profession puts him or her at a higher risk for moral corruption than most other occupations because it involves exerting power and matters of life and death. Warriors exercised the power to take or save lives, order others to take or save lives, and lead or send others to their deaths. If they take this awesome responsibility too lightly – if they lose sight of the moral significance of their actions – they risk losing their humanity and their ability to flourish in human society.[10]

Feudal knights were expected to live by the chivalric code that regulated their conduct. In 1474, the towns of the German-speaking Upper Rhine revolted against Charles the Bold, the Duke of Burgundy. To restore order, the Burgundian knight Peter von Hagenbach was empowered with civil and military powers and was dispatched to the troubled region. To say that the knight brought an iron fist would be an understatement. Placed on trial for the atrocities committed during the occupation of Breisach, von Hagenbach was found guilty of war crimes and beheaded. His crimes of murder, rape and perjury were deemed "contrary to the laws of God and man." His only plea was that he was carrying out the orders of his prince.

The Lure of Honor

In Plato's *Phaedrus*, he divides the soul into three parts. The lowest is what he terms the appetitive. This part seeks to satisfy bodily needs and pleasures. Up from that is the spirited, which includes ambition, anger, and the desire for honor. The highest is the rational, which seeks knowledge for its own sake. Then, in *The Republic*, Plato divided human beings into three classes: lovers of wisdom, lovers of honor, and lovers of gain. For Plato, warriors fall into this second category. In his estimation, soldiers were motivated by the appetitive aspect of the

---

[10] Shannon E. French, *The Code of the Warrior: Exploring Warrior Values Past and Present* (Lanham, MD: Rowman & Littlefield, 2016), 6.

soul, much like most politicians are quite often absorbed in the desire for wealth and public honor.

It was no doubt a desire for honor that led many to volunteer for a mission they had no idea would even succeed. To find just the right men he needed for his South Pole exploration, Ernest Shackleton posted the following advertisement:

Men wanted for hazardous journey. Low wages, bitter cold, long hours of complete darkness. Safe return doubtful. Honor and recognition in event of success.

In light of this, it may be asked, is the love of honor therefore a base desire? In *Henry V*, Shakespeare has King Henry energize the spirits of his haggard army with the words, "if it be a sin to covet honor, I am the most offending soul alive." Likewise, Carl von Clausewitz once observed, "Of all the passions that inspire a man in a battle, none, we have to admit, is so powerful and so constant as the longing for honor and renown." As used by Homer in the Iliad, honor is a prize to be won. When Achilles gives his reason for fighting at Troy, honor is his chief concern: "I came to make war here not because the Trojans are responsible for any wrong committed against me. I have no quarrel with them. I came to gain honor." When Agamemnon takes away Briseis, his war prize, this threatens Achilles' status as a recipient of honor. In light of these famous examples, can it therefore be said that the love of honor is a base desire?

At this point we find the beauty and simplicity of Stoicism helpful. According to Stoicism, the ultimate goal in life to is live in conformity with nature. Perhaps this is best understood in two ways. First, in regard to ourselves, this means we should live as we were designed to live. In the second sense, it may mean we are to live in accordance with natural laws. Taken together, this has several implications. Consider, whether we were born as a slave like Epictetus or like Emperor Marcus Aurelius, we should live our ultimate "best self."

Here's where I really like the Stoics. As all good thinkers, they believed one should live according to reason. As such, the Stoics sought to act in accord with nature, and sought to be resigned to their fate. In other words, their ethic was "learning to want what one gets, rather than of getting what one wants." Albeit, they did not advocate passivity. Over against the Epicureans, they sought involvement in public life (the emperor Marcus Aurelius was a Stoic). In a bigger sense, as the stoic philosopher Seneca would have it, living in conformity with nature also means submitting to the will of Providence.

In his work *On Providence*, Seneca exhorts us to seek out what we are called to do in life. For, he says, "no one finds out what he can do except by trying." The point is, the Stoics would have us enjoy honor when it comes our way, in the due diligence of our duty, but they would not have us seek honor for itself. This they termed *philotimia*. It is for this reason that Stoics make fine warriors.

In my experience, the lure of honor may be likened to a mirage. It is for this reason that I think the lure of honor, can be a base desire, that is, if we are like Achilles. In the last analysis, we are at our best when we live by honor and enjoy when it comes our way.

The Love of Honor

In classical Greek literature, honor evokes the relationship between a warrior, his god, and the land that he protects. According to General MacArthur, the soldier who is called upon to offer and to give his life for his country, is the noblest development of mankind. In this vein, Medal of Honor recipient, Army Master Sergeant, Roy Benavidez remarks, "There's a saying among us veterans. For those who have fought for it, life has a special flavor that the protected will never know."

Likewise, in a speech, on the occasion of his receiving the Medal of Honor, Army Staff Sergeant (SSG) David G. Bellavia said the following:

Why do American warriors under fire do what men have done since this nation's inception? This is a common thread that connects the militias of Lexington and Concord with the warriors of Fallujah. It's our love of nation, our way of life, and our love by those who we serve with side by side. We defend. We avenge. We sacrifice. We bleed, and we are willing to die for this unique creation: The United States of America. I am complete for having experienced that kind of sacrifice with my fellow men at arms. And those who died, they gave their life for me they gave their lives for you, and countless citizens will never know them. These men will never get the chance to experience the cycle of life, the birth and growth of their children. They shall not grow old because they chose to stand at our place and face the enemy for us. It's not enough to acknowledge the fallen by name or just inscribe their names. We must acknowledge how and why they gave their lives. Their death wasn't a random act or a splash of misfortune. These men and women voluntarily put themselves in harm's way, prepared to die, so that we may rest secured at home. They are the insurance policy that guarantees that our founding documents, our God given rights are more worthy than their own tomorrow's.

One thing SSG Bellavia reminds us of is the profession of arms exists to defend honor. And what courses through each line of his speech is his love of honor and Country. Loving honor, and living by it, we are at our best when we enjoy when it comes our way.

America's Honor

As previously mentioned, the ground floor of American Warrior Philosophy is simply a commitment to serve the Nation – to do our duty. In our American tradition, as I hope to have demonstrated, at least in some measure, honor has played a key role. The Declaration of Independence ends with these words, "With a firm Reliance on the Protection of divine Providence, we mutually pledge to each other our Lives, our Fortunes, and our sacred Honor." By finishing the Declaration with the words, "sacred honor," it's clear that our Founding Fathers rightly anchored the whole of their argument and justification for separating from Britain with that word, "honor."

One of the Founding Fathers of our Country, George Washington (1732-99), was commander in chief of the

Continental Army during the American Revolutionary War (1775-1783). He became our first president and served two terms, from 1789 to 1797. Washington was raised in colonial Virginia. As a young man, he worked as a surveyor, then fought in the French and Indian War (1754-1763). During the Revolutionary War, he led the Continental Army to victory over the British and became a national hero.

For Washington, duty itself was a privilege. In fact, upon receiving the command of the Continental Army, he said, "But lest some unlucky event should happen unfavorable to my reputation, I beg it may be remembered by every gentleman in the room that I this day declare with the utmost sincerity, I do not think myself equal to the command I am honored with."

As the revolution flared into war, American military conduct lacked a coherent strategy. Instead, the war was carried along by the momentum of events. On June 19, 1775, the Continental Congress commissioned George Washington as Commander in Chief of the Continental Army. Taking command of the Continental Army, Washington laid siege to Boston, and bombarded British ships in Boston harbor. He then proceeded south to New York City and began constructing fortifications to thwart the coming British attack.

Honor is the one word that quickens the steps of warriors down to the ages. In his general orders of July 2, 1776, Washington wrote, "The fate of unborn millions will now depend, under God, on the courage and conduct of this army. Our cruel and unrelenting enemy leaves us no choice but a brave resistance, or the most abject submission; this is all we can expect. We have therefore to resolve to conquer or die: Our country's honor calls upon us for a vigorous and manly exertion; and if we now shamefully fail, we shall become infamous to the whole world."

With the British having landed on Long Island, and the battle soon to be joined, Washington addressed his army in a solemn appeal. "The hour is fast approaching, on which the Honor and Success of this army, and the safety of our bleeding Country depend. Remember officers and Soldiers, that you are free men, fighting for the blessings of Liberty -- that slavery will be your portion, and that of your posterity, if you do not acquit yourselves like men."

Mustering some 19,000 men, 10,000 of which were militia, Washington faced General William Howe and over 25,000 British troops of the line. Suffice it to say the Battles of Long Island and White Plains did not go well. The British soundly defeated Washington's army and gained New York, which they held for the rest of the war. Despite the moving and brilliant language of the Declaration of Independence, it seemed as though it was about to go into the dustbin of history. Then with the aid of their Hessian mercenaries, the British drove Washington out of New Jersey and into Pennsylvania. On December 18, 1776, Washington wrote to his brother John:

You can form no Idea of the perplexity of my Situation. No man, I believe, ever had a greater choice of difficulties and less means to extricate himself from them. However under a full persuasion of the justice of our cause I cannot but think the prospect will brighten, although for a wise purpose it is, at present hid under a cloud.

Washington was convinced that barring a miracle, the cause of independence was all but lost. In fact, writing to his cousin in Virginia he opined, "I think the game is pretty near up." Making matters worse, Washington's army was small and was getting smaller. At his disposal, he had 2,000 Continental troops, who were regular fighting men, and an additional 2,000 militia, who were notoriously unreliable. All of which were not trained to the level of a British regular. This would be Washington's plight for the remainder of the war. Adding to his difficulties, his militia had signed on for a three-month period which was to expire on January 1, 1777.[11] Facing this deadline, and with the morale of the army at an all-time low, necessity called for Washington to make his own miracle.

On the New Jersey side of the Delaware River the British had gone into winter quarters in Trenton. Washington's spies informed him as to the disposition of the enemy. Trenton was occupied by some 1,400 Hessian soldiers under the command of Colonel Johann Gottlieb Rall. On Christmas night, with the Hessians snug in their winter quarters, Washington's 2,400 men loaded up on

---

[11] John Ferling, *Almost a Miracle: The American Victory in the War of Independence* (New York: Oxford), 2007.

barges and crossed the icy Delaware River. However, his two other columns numbering about 3,000 failed to make the crossing. Faced with a storm that lashed his army with sleet and freezing rain, and nearly three hours behind his timetable, Washington considered a withdrawal.[12] But he knew full well that if his plan failed, he and his men would be captured, and the war would be over. And so, he pressed on. His stalwart courage would soon pay off.

Surprise was complete. Falling upon the Hessians, many of which were still inebriated from the night before, Washington's army routed Rall's forces, capturing some 900. Following up on his success, Washington closed in on the British at Princeton, defeating them on January 3, 1777. With these victories, the fight for independence remained alive. Yet, the year 1777 witnessed two more of his defeats at Brandywine, and Germantown. Afterward, his army of about 10,000 went into winter quarters at Valley Forge in December 1777. This was arguably the darkest point of the revolution. In the extreme cold, and lacking adequate food and clothing, some 3,000 of these men succumbed to disease or starvation.

Yet they survived the crucible. And in the Spring of 1778, the troops who weathered the winter emerged seasoned and disciplined. Attacking Howe's successor, General Henry Clinton, Washington fought him to a draw at Monmouth in 1778, and then was victorious at Yorktown in 1781, receiving General Cornwallis' sword, and the British surrender. This is not to say the war was

---

[12] David Hackett Fisher, *Washington's Crossing* (New York: Oxford), 2006.

won in the North. Cornwallis was in Yorktown to begin with because of his defeats at the hands of patriots in the South. All told, Washington's record was four defeats, one draw, and three victories; not exactly the combat record you would expect from a victorious general. Yet Washington was a great general because without him there would not have been any American history.

Besides the battles he fought, Washington also faced many other threats to the fledgling republic. As the War of Independence was winding down, on May 22, 1782, he received a letter as he was encamped at Newburgh, New York. Known as the Newburgh Letter, the correspondence was from Continental Army Colonel Lewis Nicola. The letter proposed that Washington should become the King of the United States. Nicola was spokesman for a certain group of Army officers who threatened to take over the government if they were not paid. In his reply, dated the same day, Washington gave a clear answer,

Sir, with a mixture of great surprise and astonishment I have read with attention the sentiments you have submitted to my perusal. Be assured sir, no occurrence in the course of the war, has given me more painful sensations than your information of there being such ideas existing in the Army as you have expressed, and I must view with abhorrence, and reprehend with severity... Let me conjure you then, if you have any regard for your Country, concern for yourself or posterity or respect for me, to banish these thoughts from your mind, and never communicate, as from yourself, or anyone else, a sentiment of the like nature.

Chapter 2: Honor

No doubt, a lessor man would have faltered at the point of being so highly honored. But being the man of honor that he was, and seeing himself as a servant to our Nation, though he had ample opportunity, Washington viewed with abhorrence any idea of himself being made king. Then, following his Army service he said, "Having now finished the work assigned me, I retire from the great theatre of Action."

Washington then went on to preside over the convention that wrote the US Constitution in 1787. Then, two years later, he became America's first president. Realizing that the way he handled the job would impact how future presidents approached the position, he handed down a legacy of strength, integrity and national purpose. In his first year as president, Washington said, "It is the duty of all nations, to acknowledge the Providence of Almighty God, to obey his will, to be grateful for his benefits, and humbly to implore his protection and favor." Speaking of the ways of Providence, he wrote, "By the all-powerful dispensations of Providence, I have been protected beyond all human probability and expectation; for I had four bullets through my coat, and two horses shot under me, yet escaped unhurt."

Cincinnatus was the Roman senator who was twice summoned to become dictator of Rome to defeat its enemies. Afterwards he relinquished the office and returned to farming. Like Cincinnatus, when he felt his work had been accomplished, Washington retired to Mount Vernon. He died there less than three years after leaving office at age sixty-seven. Of the many things we learn from Washington's life, perhaps the greatest is his mindset, that of a servant. He always envisioned himself as a servant of the State, and a guardian of the Republic. Oh, that all American warriors had this great mindset! On January 8, 1790, in one of his final addresses to the Congress, having witnessed the birth of the Nation, he so strongly fought to see become free, in solemn tones, he said, "To be prepared for war is one of the most effectual means of preserving peace."

Principles of Honor

Socrates once remarked, "Let him who would move the world first move himself." To help you do that, I want to share ten warrior principles, two per virtue. Here are two principles: One that reminds us of what to know, and one of what to do.

Know: <u>Sowing virtue, reaps honor</u>. Honor has an eternal quality and dictates how things are to be said and done. This was true 2,000 years ago, its true today, and it'll be true tomorrow.

Do: <u>Be professional. Be polite. Be prepared to kill</u>. The inspiration for this comes from Marine Corps General James Mattis who once said, "Be polite, be professional, but have a plan to kill everybody you meet." Our mission is to deploy, engage, and destroy, the enemies of the United States in close combat.

The dictates of honor require these activities to be done in an honorable fashion, so as to keep our honor clean. Unfortunately, there have been numerous atrocities in our Nation's history. Among these was the infamous atrocity at My Lai, South Vietnam. On March 16, 1968, a company of American soldiers brutally massacred most of the women, children, and old men in the village of My Lai. This unspeakable event received national news.

Taking part in a larger search-and-destroy sweep, the newly formed Task Force Barker, of 1st Battalion, 20th Infantry Regiment, 23rd Infantry Division, expected to wipe out the remnants of the National Liberation Front's (NLF's) 48th Local Force Battalion. Following an initial artillery barrage and helicopter gunfire softening, the 100-man Task Force Barker began a ground sweep. First Platoon, C Company, led by Second Lieutenant William L. Calley, Jr. were in the vanguard, and were the first to make contact with the enemy in the hamlet of My Lai. As reported to the press, the day's operation successfully bagged some 128 NLF dead, with no American casualties. In reality, more than 500 people were slaughtered, including young girls and women who were raped and mutilated before being killed. The event truly marks a black page in American history.

Massacres such as My Lai leave us with many questions. How could such atrocities be perpetrated by American fighting men? As it came out in the wash, C

Chapter 2: Honor

Company had suffered their fair share of casualties during the Tet Offensive, a Viet Cong surge that was launched less than two months before. A fatal coalescence of venting their pent-up rage, dehumanizing their enemy, and seeing the people as Viet Cong sympathizers, led C Company to "do" the village. There are certainly lines that are never to be crossed. The murder of civilians is indeed one of them. Whatever honor Calley and his men walked into My Lai with, they certainly left it in the dust. Lieutenant Calley was later court-martialed.

Honor is the quality that is difficult to describe but easily recognized. Honor empowers warriors to do incredible things. It was for honor that Leonidas in his 300 stood against myriads. The four other virtues are built on the foundation of honor. Now these are abstract ideas but when we read the accounts of uncommon valor which is articulated in citation after citation of the Medal of Honor recipients, then we see how this metaphysical sacred quality enters the realm of sweat, pain, and blood to produce prodigious results.

As we go on to discuss the other virtues, I would be remiss not to remind us once again that America was founded on the principles of honor, which our Founding Fathers believed to be sacred. In the Nineteenth Century, Alexis de Tocqueville, in his work *Democracy in America* said this of the United States:

I sought for the greatness and genius of America in her commodious harbors and her ample rivers, and it was not there. I sought for the greatness and genius of America in her fertile fields and boundless forests, and it was not there. I sought for the greatness and genius of America in her rich mines and her vast world commerce, and it was not there. I sought for the greatness and genius of America in her public school system and her institutions of learning, and it was not there. I sought for the greatness and genius of America in her democratic Congress and her matchless Constitution, and it was not there. Not until I went into the churches of America and heard her pulpits flame with righteousness did I understand the secret of her genius and power. America is great because she is good, and if America ever ceases to be good, she will cease to be great.

Tocqueville's simple point rings true. America is great because she is good. If she is no longer good, she'll no longer be great.

Echoing the sentiment of Vegetius, that "the decline and eventual fall of Rome was due primarily to the warrior class straying away from their ideals," these are virtues every American should have. If this country is to remain strong and free, then we all need to go back to our core values that caused this Country to become a strong nation.

Chapter 2: Honor

Introspection

I have purposely bookended each of the following five chapters with five introspective questions. These are designed to promote professional growth:

1. What am I most proud of?

2. If I was to die today, what would I regret not doing?

3. What does it mean to leave a legacy?

4. What would my epitaph read?

5. What does it mean to die well?

The Battle of Bunker Hill, June 17, 1776.

3

Integrity

"Better the fool who walks in his integrity than one perverse in his ways, though he be rich." – Proverbs 28:6

Among the most basic human desires is to fit in. The need for acceptance is instinctive. Warriors are no different. This intrinsic need at times can be a challenge to the dictates of honor. What this means is, more so than others, warriors are susceptible to group pressure, and may be tempted to commit actions they would otherwise not normally do of their own volition. This underscores the need for awareness of how social pressures and situational forces can have influence on us.

In his book, *Ordinary Men*, Christopher Browning tells the true story of the Nazi Police force, Reserve Police Battalion 101 and the part it played in the final solution, the plan for the systematic elimination of Jews, in Poland. Arriving in the Lublin district of Poland, the battalion received its orders for a "special action." The nature of this mission was not specified in their written orders. While the men were led to believe their task would amount to guard duty, they discovered this "special action" amounted to the mass execution of Polish Jews by firing squad. Arriving in the village of Józefów in the early morning, Battalion 101's commander, Major Wilhelm Trapp addressed his assembled troops. After explaining the grizzly assignment, he gave the men an offer: those not up to the task could opt out. Ten voiced their desire to do so. Those who stayed took part in the murder that followed.

Systematically, Reserve Battalion 101 cleared the village of Jews. They sent the most able-bodied to work camps, while the majority were chauffeured to their deaths in the forest. At a reception area, another element of the battalion stood by. These men were given a quick class on where to shoot a man. Soon the first trucks arrived. The Jews were ordered to lie face down in rows. Then, on command, their executioners stepped forward and fired a shot into the necks of their victims at pointblank range. "Except for a midday break, the shooting proceeded without interruption."

Reflecting on what made some men stay, Browning opines, "When Trapp first made his offer early in the morning, the real nature of the action had just been announced and time to think and react had been very short. Only a dozen men had instinctively seized the moment to step out, turn in their rifles, and thus excuse themselves from the subsequent killing."[1]

It is worth mentioning that the men of Reserve Police Battalion 101 were "ordinary men." They were working-class civilians from Hamburg, and had not volunteered for the SS. As such, they were not particularly strong advocates of Nazism. What is clear is, in the face of shame from their fellow policemen, a minority bravely refused to participate in the murderous work. A threat of shame and a pressure to conform led the majority to stay. These fell prey to what Philip Zimbardo describes as "the power of situational forces over individual behavior."[2]

By the end of 13 July 1942, the Battalion had slaughtered 1500 Jews in seventeen hours. Documenting their first mission, Browning recounts that copious amounts of alcohol was provided to keep the "work" going. He further notes that the lack of training made the work "messy," adding the gory detail that the men's uniforms dripped "wet with brain matter and blood." The Battalion would go on to repeat this dastardly deed in thirteen more villages, and in the end would account for the deaths of some 83,000 Jews. As Browning goes on to

---

[1] Christopher R. Browning, *Ordinary Men: Reserve Police Battalion 101 and the Final Solution in Poland* (New York: Harper Collins, 1992), 61.
[2] Philip Zimbardo, *The Lucifer Effect: Understanding How Good People Turn Evil* (New York: Random House, 2008).

say, those who took part in the bloody business suffered severe psychological damage.

As demonstrated by the brave minority who opted out of this collective murder, integrity overpowers shame. There was simply no honor in the deeds of the majority who remained. For them, situational forces, and group dynamics such as dehumanization, blind obedience, and moral disengagement, worked in concert to make monsters out of these decent men.[3] These factors coalesced into a system that created the toxic and deadly situation. To use Philip Zimbardo's expression, it was a bad barrel that created bad apples.

The Imperial Japanese Army invaded Shanghai in the fall of 1937. In the ensuing urban fight, they met strong resistance. Casualties were high and Japanese morale plummeted. Nonetheless, the Japanese rapid advance caught Chang Kai-Shek's Nationalist Army off balance, leaving the city of Nanking undefended. On 13 December 1937, the Japanese 10th Army, commanded by General Iwane Matsui, entered Nanking. What followed was six weeks of unrestrained barbarity.

The rapacious Japanese Army butchered some 300,000 Chinese, and raped an estimated 20,000 to 80,000 women, many of whom were killed afterward. As recounted by author Iris Chang, "Many soldiers went beyond rape to disembowel women, slice off their breasts, nail them alive to walls. Fathers were forced to rape their daughters, and sons their mothers, as other family

---

[3] *The Lucifer Effect*, 8.

members watched. So sickening was the spectacle that even the Nazis in the city we're horrified, one proclaiming the matter to be the work of bestial machinery."[4]

Shiro Azuma, a Japanese soldier who participated in the massacre, recounts the motivation behind the work of this "bestial machinery":

We had fun killing Chinese. When we caught some Chinese civilians, we either buried them alive, or pushed them into a fire, or beat them to death with clubs. When they were half dead, we pushed them into ditches and burned them, torturing them to death. Everyone gets his entertainment this way. It's like killing dogs and cats... We were taught that we were a superior race since we lived only for the sake of a human god— our emperor. But the Chinese were not. So, we held nothing but contempt for them... We sent out trucks into the city to seize women. Once we captured them, we took turns raping them. We did not spare old women or young girls of this treatment. Once we were finished raping them, we always stabbed and killed them. When we were raping them, we looked at them like they were women. But when we killed them, we just thought of them as something like a pig. We did everything for the sake of the Emperor, the raping, the killing, everything.

Clearly, the Japanese dehumanized their Chinese victims as civilians were used for bayonet practice, "decapitation contests," and rifle marksmanship "training." Space will not permit a full commentary. Suffice it to say that Japanese atrocities committed against the innocent civilians in China and in other parts

---

[4] Iris Chang, *The Rape of Nanking: The Forgotten Holocaust of World War II* (New York: Perseus, 1997), 6.

of the so-called Japanese "Greater East Asia Co-Prosperity Sphere" were wanton acts of depravity. It may be said that the war leaders of Japan appealed to the ideals of Bushido yet failed to inculcate them in the training regimens of their soldiers. The Bushido of the Imperial Japanese Army of WWII bore little resemblance to the Bushido of medieval Japan. Albeit, echoes of feudal Bushido were seen in the many seppuku-style suicide charges and kamikaze dive bombs throughout the war.

In chapter one, I mentioned the Bushido code. Clearly, the Rape of Nanking is an example of the dangers of merely assuming everyone knows and lives out warrior virtues. That this despicable act of cowardly brutality impinged upon Japanese honor is seen in the fact that as late as 1990 Japanese government officials categorically denied the reality of the Rape of Nanking. Japanese Congressman Shintaro Ishihara was quoted as saying the whole ordeal was "a story made-up by the Chinese."

To cite one other example, as the Second World War was coming to an end in Europe, a bloody and brutal battle was erupting in Berlin. The Soviet Red Army had advanced into the heartland of Nazi Germany. On 22 April 1945, the first wave of Soviet troops entered Berlin. Fighting street to street, they shot every man they saw, even old men and young boys, but they left the women alone. The Russians would lose some 80,000 men taking Berlin. The second wave that followed, did all the plundering and raping. Completely lacking any discipline, these vengeful Soviet troops drank heavily as they pillaged and raped their way across the city.

According to the Soviet war correspondent Natalya Gesse, Red Army soldiers raped German females from eight to eighty years old. The women of Berlin were being treated as spoils of war. It's recounted that not even nuns were spared, and a hospital full of women who had just given birth were also raped. Many women found themselves the victims of repeated rapes. Some as many as sixty to seventy times.[5]

Feeling that their national pride had been violated by the German invasion of Barbarossa (1941), in their minds, Soviet soldiers believed themselves justified in their actions. Before the Battle of Berlin would be over, about 22,000 civilians were killed and an estimated 100,000 German women and girls were raped.

During WWII, Allied troops also engaged in such despicable acts. Following the Battle of Monte Cassino in Italy, between Naples and Rome, French Colonial troops, mainly Moroccan Goumiers, raped some 2,000 women, along with six hundred men and boys. Complaints were taken to the French commander who merely laughed saying, "This is war. A year or two ago, the Italian soldiers were doing the same thing in Africa." American and British troops were likewise guilty, albeit in isolated doses. In his book, *Taken by Force*, J. Robert Lilly cites numerous examples of American soldiers raping German women and girls. He estimates the number of these atrocities, some gang rapes at gunpoint, committed by US

---

[5] William I. Hitchcock, *The Struggle for Europe: The Turbulent History of a Divided Continent, 1945 to the Present* (New York: Anchor Books, 2004).

servicemen to be over 11,000. The author argues that such sexual violence is an "inherent feature of military culture," as well as a "means of revenge."

It is a known fact that until the modern age, and sadly, including the modern age, nearly every conquering army has pillaged and raped the citizens of its vanquished foe. As author Philip Freeman suggests, "Armies in the ancient world firmly believed it was their natural right to pillage any city they encountered. As for captive women, in the minds of the soldiers they were nothing more than the spoils of war and were to be treated as such." Citing an example, Philip Freeman recounts the psychological state of Alexander's army following its seven-month siege of Tyre:

The ferocity of the slaughter was staggering. The Macedonians had spent seven long months laboring to take the stubborn town. They had seen many of their friends crushed by stones hurled from the walls or burned to death by firebombs. They were angry, exhausted, and passionately hated the people of Tyre for putting them through hell.[6]

I would argue that the above examples of vengeful armies of WWII were motivated by the same sentiment. Due to the despicable nature of such crimes, many histories either pass over them in silence, or relegate them to footnotes. I have taken the time to highlight the effects that social forces can have on individuals. Such psychological effects can lead men to commit acts that:

---

[6] Philip Freeman, *Alexander the Great* (New York: Simon & Schuster, 2011), 278.

(1) are crimes of obedience that follow immoral orders, or (2) acts that conform to group norms which "normalize" wanton acts of depravity, or (3) are crimes of inaction, and (4) moral disengagement, standing aloof from what is morally right.

Before the advent of global positioning devices (GPS), when you were doing land navigation and became lost, what you did is you would go back to your last known point. I would argue that while you can gain more honor, be more loyal, more temperant, and courageous, integrity is the only virtue that is constant. As a warrior, you will undoubtedly be faced with many challenges, and dilemmas. Whenever you get lost, integrity is the "known point." That has to be true, or you will be truly lost.

Definition

In olden times, a man would rather sacrifice his life than his word. If honor is a sacred prize that has an individual and corporate quality that is expressed, shared, and guarded; and if loyalty is the sacred bond between the brotherhood of warriors, then integrity is what keeps honor intact. This is reflected in the meaning of *the* word "integrity." The ancient Greeks did not have a word for it. Our word in English comes to us from the Latin *integer* and literally means "intact." At the simplest level, what integrity does is it keeps one's honor intact. Similarly, the modern Greek word *akeraiotita* means "state of being undivided."

86

Chapter 3: Integrity

The Preeminence of Integrity

Integrity is essential to a warrior's character, discipline, and conduct. Integrity means doing the hard right over the easy wrong; even when no one is watching. Integrity characterizes the entire person. Integrity only burdens the dishonest man.

One of the most powerful men in the world was renowned for his integrity. Marcus Aurelias was the Emperor of the Roman Empire from 161-180 AD. As Roman Emperor, Marcus Aurelius had absolute power of life and death over everyone in the known world. According to the English philosopher Lord Acton, great men are almost always bad men. As such, "Power tends to corrupt and absolute power corrupts absolutely." Marcus Aurelius is among these rare exceptions.

As emperor, he possessed unlimited power over the known world for nineteen years. He could engage in the most outlandish enterprises. He could have sex with anyone he so desired, as often as he desired. He could have gone off on a nineteen-year drinking bender. Marcus Aurelius is instead an exception to Lord Acton's dictum.

While Marcus Aurelius is remembered as one of the five good emperors, defeating the German tribes, facing the devastating consequences of the Antonine Plague, he is perhaps best remembered for his stoicism. In his estimation, you should "never esteem anything as of advantage to you that will make you break your word or lose your self-respect."[7] Extolling the virtue of integrity, the ancient Greek philosopher Heraclitus likewise once observed that it was this virtue that is in fact the light which guides our way.

I was privileged to serve in the US Army Special Forces for eighteen years. For the past thirteen years I have been privileged to instruct Special Forces soldiers. Whenever I ask a Green Beret cadre what the most important virtue is in a student, they invariably answer integrity. Underscoring its importance, the Special Forces Creed includes the words, "I pledge to uphold the honor and integrity of all I am, in all I do."

While I'm no Marcus Aurelius, on more than one occasion, I have been challenged to do the hard right over the easy wrong. It happened in the spring of 1997. I was serving in 1st Special Forces Group as an Engineer Sergeant on ODA 154 (now ODA 1224). My Team Sergeant, David Samano, informed me to prepare for the E-7 board. If I wanted to get promoted, I needed to get my ducks in a row.

So, I went to the S-1 shop who handled personnel records. The clerk handed me my microfiche and I proceeded to survey my military record on a giant box known as a microfiche reader. These now obsolete machines condensed one's 201 File down to a flat piece of film containing microphotographs of all your awards and orders for promotion, etc.

---

[7] Marcus Aurelius, *Meditations*.

Chapter 3: Integrity

As I sat at a table and perused my files, I discovered orders that awarded me the Ranger tab. This came as a shock. Three years earlier I attended the Ranger Course but returned as a failure. I had been recycled in Darby, and the Mountain phase, spent over a hundred days tormented by the summer heat of Georgia, only to walk off the trail on our grueling 15-mile ruck march back into Camp Merrill. The injury to my knee sent me packing.

I have to admit, staring at that screen gave me some ideas. The idea of going back to Benning to get that short tab, that had evaded me, permeated my thoughts for the previous three years. And here was a set of orders that could change all of that. Without checking the remainder of my record, I promptly turned off the machine and asked the clerk to print off several copies of the orders awarding me the coveted tab.

Folding them up, I cached them away in my cargo pocket. The rest of the day I spent daydreaming of how that glorious cloth would look beneath my Special Forces long tab. But these afternoon hours of fantasy were disturbed by my troubled conscience. I went to the men's room, closed the stall, and read the orders again. Some idiot clerk had made a mistake at Benning. I didn't earn that tab. But in the flood of names that crossed his desk, he nonetheless typed my name on a set of orders authorizing me to wear a tab I didn't earn. I went home but couldn't get the thought off my mind.

The next morning, I went back to S-1. I asked for a DA Form 4187, a personnel action form. I used it to request attendance at the next available Ranger Course. I also handed the clerk the set of orders that awarded me the Ranger Tab and asked for them to be revocated. The clerk looked at me as though I had an extra head. He took the papers. A minute later he returned with his supervisor, a staff sergeant. In light of the paradox, the supervisor asked for clarification.

As I explained the matter, they both smiled and shook their heads as though I was the dumbest man they had ever met. Following a good laugh, they processed the forms, and I went back to Benning in the fall. I went on to earn the Ranger Tab. And looking back, that was one of the hardest but best decisions I ever made. Perhaps no one would have known. But I would know. And that made all the difference. Now, I've made a lot of mistakes in my life, but thank God that was not one of them.

The Paucity of Integrity

Among the tumultuous events that occurred in the year 2022, billionaire Sam Bankman-Fried, founder and CEO of cryptocurrency FTX, made headlines by being accused of defrauding US investors of billions. On December 13, 2022, Federal prosecutors charged Bankman-Fried with multiple counts of wire fraud, securities fraud, money laundering, and campaign finance violations. The man who was lauded by Fortune Magazine as the next Warren Buffet, diverted investors funds to another company, without their knowledge, made lavish real estate purchases, and huge political donations. His actions imploded FTX, leading the company to file for bankruptcy, leaving millions of people unable to access their funds.

As I've learned in the military, you can train someone virtually in anything. Albeit, as a man learns and applies these skills, the one constant will be that man's sense of integrity. This raises an interesting point. In the military, we train men on all manner of weapons systems and technology that potentially can annihilate whole civilizations but then assume that these men all have the values, beliefs and norms that will make them great soldiers who will execute their duties with integrity. Sadly, I've seen this to be a false assumption. I've discovered many highly trained immoral men.

Considering again the Stoic Emperor, arguably, not many of us could maintain our integrity if faced with such power and wealth at our disposal. According to recent statistics, the estimated number of those who cheat on their taxes in America was 1.6 million people. These million and a half people cost the government a staggering $270 billion. What these figures don't include are tax returns that were fudged. Perhaps so many cheat because they reason, "hey everybody else is doing it. Why can't I?"

As Brett McKay has aptly said, studies show, "big moral mistakes are invariably preceded by smaller ones. The slide towards ethical ambiguity begins with little, seemingly insignificant choices." Having the privilege to serve in our Nation's most elite units, one thing stands out in this discussion of integrity. And that is, of all the soldiers I have seen kicked out of these elite units, the majority were for moral failings. At the heart of such failings was an integrity issue.

As I've argued, our American values come to us from essentially three sources: the Bible, The Declaration of Independence, and the Constitution of the United States. Any soldier who has been in a unit for any length of time has seen fellow soldiers punished for not abiding by our values. Most enter the military already having these values. However, many who are invariably later punished under the Uniform Code of Military Justice (UCMJ), enter the military not already having a set of values that are in line with established norms. To fix this, the Army has taken various steps at reinforcing these age-old values. Take for instance the dog-tags that express the Army values.

Abu Ghraib Prisoner Abuse

As history demonstrates, the United States military has suffered from scandals and abuses that stem from, more often than not, personal integrity problems. Examples are legion. As a famous one, take for instance the Abu Ghraib prisoner abuse scandal. The story broke on 28 April 2004 when photographs showing US Army soldiers abusing Iraqi detainees made their way to the public media. The story soon made national headlines. Several reserve soldiers from the 327th Military Police battalion were given positions for which they were untrained, unsupervised, with no management.

Chapter 3: Integrity

Seven reservists, with zero training, were placed in charge over about two hundred Iraqi detainees. Operating in concert with these reservists, during the night shift, were a mixed group of CIA and contract interrogators. Wanting to know about al Qaeda and the insurgency that was destabilizing Iraq, these reservists were encouraged to help elicit information.

As the insurgency gained momentum, the Coalition Troops of Operation Iraqi Freedom nabbed suspected operatives. The prison soon swelled to nearly a thousand detainees. To "prepare" them for the following day's questioning, these seven reservist soldiers created an environment they hoped would elicit the needed information. A "little shop of horrors" was then created. The lights were dimmed, and sound effects were added to create a dungeon-like atmosphere. The detainees were stripped naked.

The situation being what it was, particular dynamics of moral disengagement, and conformity began to take effect as the detainees were dehumanized. The shift leader, Staff Sergeant Ivan Frederick, began to take pictures of the abuse that unfolded. Among the reservist military police guards in the prison was Private First Class Lynndie England, who had her twenty-first birthday while there. Lynndie and another guard, Specialist Charles Graner, had an affair. Playfully they subjected detainees to sexual, physical, and psychological abuse.

In photos that reveal what Philip Zimbardo referred to as "digital documented depravity," naked detainees were bitten by dogs, shot with non-lethal ammunition, forced to form human pyramids, one was led around naked by a leash, others were forced to masturbate, and even perform sexual acts on each other.

With responsibility over hundreds of Iraqi prisoners, these American soldiers "engaged in unimaginable forms of torture against civilians they were supposed to be guarding."[8] These actions humiliated the military. In response, seventeen soldiers and officers were removed from duty. A further eleven were charged with dereliction of duty, maltreatment, aggravated assault and battery.

In his book, *The Lucifer Effect*, Philip Zimbardo demonstrates how our personalities can change depending on situations. Obedience to authority is among the most valued traits in a soldier. In a sense, at least for Staff Sergeant Ivan Frederick, the power of situational forces led him to commit and be complicit in sordid "crimes of obedience." With US military personnel dying every day in roadside bombs, Frederick is recounted as feeling it was his duty to permit such abuse to go on. Observing how good people can do evil things, Zimbardo notes, "The line between good and evil is permeable and almost anyone can be induced to cross it when pressured by situational forces."[9]

---

[8] Zimbardo, *The Lucifer Effect*, 18.
[9] Ibid.

Chapter 3: Integrity

Our national values are what made America a free country and the most powerful nation on the face of the earth. With such power comes great responsibility. The responsibility of the American warrior class is to act appropriately toward the other nations of the world, friend or foe.

The Price of Integrity

Now, it may be slightly apocryphal, but a story of one of America's great warriors demonstrates the payoff of integrity. As legend has it, Francis Marion was attending a party hosted by a fellow Patriot officer, Captain Alexander McQueen. To encourage his guests to consume large amounts of alcohol, McQueen had the doors of the house locked. As a Christian man, desiring to avoid the sin of drunkenness, Marion's sense of integrity prompted him to jump from a second story window. He hobbled home with a broken ankle. However, because he was recovering at home, he was not nabbed along with the other 5,000 Patriots who were there when Charleston fell on May 12, 1780. Marion went on to lead his own partisan war in the swamps of South Carolina. His bloody adventures helped win the Revolutionary War.

Integrity is priceless and involves having the strength of character to do what is right. This may involve taking an unpopular or controversial stand for what one knows is right. Doing so can damage one's career. In fact, many of the very best careers have been cut short by taking a stand for integrity.

Consider John Paul Vann. The main character of Neil Sheehan's *Bright Shining Lie*, Vann was an Army Lieutenant Colonel who served in Vietnam, and among the first to realize the American strategy being waged there was going the wrong way. Now, John Paul Vann was not known to be a perfect man at any stretch, however, he couldn't stomach the progress of the war, and felt it was ill-fated. Instead of winning the allegiance of the people of South Vietnam, the American strategy was that of attrition, irrespective of civilian casualties. His integrity would not allow him to go on as though he didn't see the writing on the wall. He didn't see a way for the United States to defeat the Viet Cong the way the war was being prosecuted, so he decided to resign his commission. Vann did what was right which was to his hurt.

Two years later, in 1965, Vann returned to Vietnam. This time as a civilian pacification officer. Under his leadership, a new counterinsurgency program flourished. Entitled Civil Operations and Rural Development Support (CORDS), this program systematically strangled the life of the Viet Cong. Although highly successful, the CORDS counterinsurgency project, proved to be in the estimation of its first leader, Robert W. Komer, "too little, too late." Unfortunately, Komer was right. The US withdrew from Vietnam in 1972, and the South Vietnamese republic fell to the Communists in 1975. Vann died in a helicopter crash before the end of the war. However we see him, Vann's integrity would not allow him to go on knowing what he knew. I see him as a man of integrity that was troubled by what he felt was military malpractice. It may be said that integrity checks us, barring us from certain actions that our soul deems unrighteous.

On another occasion, my integrity happily got the better of me. It happened in the Spring of 2006. It was about ninety days into a rotation with the Special Forces unit I was serving with. Basing our operations out of the so-called Green Zone, we were like vampires: We'd do our hits at night and sleep during the day. Our mission was to kill or capture Al Qaeda in Iraq (AQI), along with other assorted bad guys. We stayed busy. Following ninety-days' worth of business, including what I like to call "tactical pilfering," unbeknownst to me, my team had acquired quite a trove of Iraqi dinar. What I didn't know was that my boss was having these Iraqi dinars exchanged for Ben Franklins. About ten days prior to our scheduled return to the States, I got a knock on my barracks room door. My boss, handed me a bag of $5800 and said, "This is your cut." I stood speechless thinking "What the hell did you just say?"

I had worked my butt off getting to this point. I didn't know what to say or what to do. Without so much as a question, I respectfully took the bag and closed the door. Everything I had ever heard about integrity now came to me in a torrent like a Southern Baptist fire and brimstone preacher. I sat pensively in my barracks room. I imagined all I could do with the money. My wife could go on that Adriatic cruise she always wanted. I could do some much-needed repairs on the house. The possibilities were endless. These thoughts however were punctuated by the pangs of my troubled conscience.

I knew this was blood money. The guys we'd been killing were bomb makers. They were not just nice folks donating to the cause. They were slaughtering 101st guys with their IEDs. The money no doubt had a hand in bringing in foreign fighters, no doubt as far way as Chechnya and Libya. That money was now in a bag in my shaving kit. Suffice it to say I didn't sleep at all that night. Perhaps what troubled me the most was what my fellow warriors would think about me if I didn't take the money. I had worked so hard to get on that team. I didn't want anything to jeopardize that. But I had to do what I felt was right. In the end, that desire took over and made my decision for me.

Following a casual breakfast, I walked to my team leader's room. After politely handing him the bag of money I said, "I will happily flow into rooms with you, and make people's heads calzones, but I cannot take this money." He looked at me as though I was the dumbest guy he'd ever met. Then, without saying a word, he smiled and closed the door. In an instant, the weight of the problem that had cost me a night's sleep lifted off my conscience. The interesting thing is, I didn't have to worry about this that long because that night I was shot in the neck; a story all on its own. I didn't know at the time that would be my last night in Baghdad. The situation was later resolved when I was quietly moved to another team. Apparently, my skills were needed elsewhere.

Looking back, I have no regrets. This experience caused me to learn an important lesson regarding integrity. Our fellow warriors will forgive and forget an error in judgment, but not a lack of integrity. Integrity is priceless. We would do well to lose everything else to retain it.

Principles of Integrity

The virtue of integrity requires warriors to do things an honorable way. To be sure, as Albert Camus once put it, "Integrity needs no rules." Nonetheless, two principles here:

Know: <u>Integrity keeps honor intact.</u>

Do: <u>Do what is right, even to your own hurt.</u>

According to President Dwight D. Eisenhower, "The supreme quality for leadership is unquestionably integrity." In the last analysis, integrity is hard won and easily lost. Few things are as sad as a man who breaks his own integrity. Consider the many promising careers that have been cut short for integrity issues.

Chapter 3: Integrity

One of C. S. Lewis's most memorable essays is entitled "The Inner Ring." In it, Lewis describes the experience and desire of all of us at various stages of life. We all desire to be accepted. The desire to be "in" can make you say and do things you normally would or should not do or say. This desire, "the lure of the inner ring," can be disastrous, especially if we feel compelled to compromise our integrity to fit in and be accepted within the "inner ring" of whatever group that matters most to us. The bottom line is if you get "in," the initial rush of excitement will not last. Sooner or later, there will be yet another "inner ring" to enter. The inner ring is really a mirage. Besides, if those we aspire to rub elbows with are content with us violating integrity, they are simply not worth associating with.

Introspection

I have purposely bookended each chapter with five introspective questions. These are designed to promote professional growth:

1. What does the word integrity mean to you?

2. Have you ever suffered for doing the right thing?

3. How well do you really know yourself, your strengths and weaknesses?

4. Do others consider you trustworthy?

5. Have you ever fabricated something on your resume?

Major General Benedict Arnold rallying American troops at Saratoga, Oct 7, 1777.

4

Loyalty

"Nothing is more noble; nothing is more venerable." – Cicero

A good name is hard won and easily tarnished. Once held in high esteem, the name Benedict Arnold has now become virtually the definition of a traitor. The most infamous turncoat in American history, however, was once one of the most skilled and valorous Patriot officers of the American Revolution. He served the Patriot cause with conspicuous bravery, ensuring that the Declaration of Independence would amount to more than just bold words. By virtue of his contributions to the cause of liberty, the French were convinced to enter the war against Britain. Why this once-ardent hero of the American Revolution became its most dishonored traitor is an obvious question of loyalty. On a deeper level, it's also one of selfless service. In the end, it seems that Arnold betrayed his Country because he felt that his sacrifices were unappreciated. In a letter to Benedict Arnold, dated September 14, 1775, George Washington wrote, "Every post is honorable in which a man can serve his country." As time would tell, Washington's good advice fell on deaf ears.

As a great battlefield commander, Arnold was aggressive and talented. It is an understatement to say that without his contribution, it's debatable whether the United States would even exist. Three episodes stand out. After the Battles of Lexington and Concord, he joined forces with Ethan Allen and took Fort Ticonderoga. With the capture of the fort, the Patriots gained the guns that would eventually cause the British to evacuate Boston. Next, in 1776, drawing from his experience as a sea trader, he built one of the first American naval fleets. Cobbling together some fifteen ships and gunboats, he engaged the British Navy at the Battle of Valcour Island in Lake Champlain. This action stalled the British advance, giving Washington time to prepare Patriot defenses in New York. Following this engagement, Arnold was hailed as a hero.

Perhaps his greatest contribution to the war occurred during the Battles at Saratoga. In 1777, British forces under General John Burgoyne fought the army of General Horatio Gates to a near stand-off. It was perhaps at Saratoga that Benedict Arnold fought the most savagely, leading to a decisive Patriot victory. That outcome kept the cause for American independence alive and convinced the French to enter the war against Britain.

Badly wounded, having been shot in the left leg while leading a charge, Arnold was appointed military governor of Philadelphia. It was then that things began to go south for him when those influential in the city began a campaign to destroy his reputation. Things got so bad that Arnold was brought up on charges that lead to his court martial. Though he was later exonerated, the tarnish to his hard-earned reputation was debilitating. Having become disillusioned, feeling that the cause had betrayed him, he opens negotiations with the British in New York.

A possibility for Arnold to return to the glories of the battlefield presented itself when Washington offered him command of the left wing of the Continental Army. The scorned Arnold however asks for the command of West Point. While there, Arnold began secretly communicating with British Major André, providing him inside information, not just about the fort and its defenses, but about American strategy for the war. On September 25, 1780, his plot to betray the Hudson Valley fortress was exposed when André was captured. Having successfully evaded capture, Arnold returned to the field of battle wearing a British uniform, leading brutal attacks against Patriot communities. He burned New London,

Connecticut and later captured Richmond, destroying much-needed supply houses, foundries, and mills.

After Cornwallis fought Greene at Guildford Court House, he came north to Virginia, and then proceeded east to the coast. There, Cornwallis was directed by General Clinton to build a base and await reinforcements. While there, Arnold, who was temporarily in command of British forces, recommended to Cornwallis to locate such a base away from the coast. Ironically, Cornwallis rebuffed Arnold, promptly dug in at Yorktown on the coast, and was later bottled up by the French fleet and surrendered.

If Arnold had been mortally wounded at Saratoga, his name would have been enshrined through the land. Tragically, Arnold betrayed his Country for what he perceived to be a more honorable post. Now, nearly 250 years after he defected to the British, Major General Benedict Arnold remains among the most vilified figures in American history.[1]

The tragic story of Benedict Arnold reminds us that loyalty for one's brothers outweighs a desire for self-promotion and even preservation. Though an excellent warrior, his betrayal rendered his hard-won prestige virtually nonexistent. A visitor to the battlefield of Saratoga can be impressed by the 155-foot obelisk that commemorates the American victory. On its four sides, honoring the four American commanders responsible for

---

[1] Stephen Brumwell, Turncoat: Benedict Arnold and the Crisis of American Liberty (Yale University Press, 2018), xiii.

the victory, are four niches. Three display statutes of General Horatio Gates, General Phillip Schuyler and Colonel Daniel Morgan. The fourth niche, which would have depicted Arnold, remains empty. A deserved omission. Sadly, the man who was once called "the most brilliant soldier of the Continental Army," whose leadership at Saratoga won for his countrymen the decisive battle of the American Revolution, and for himself the rank of Major General, he would spend his wanning years in utter infamy.

Definition

The word loyalty in the Greek is *eleos,* and literally means faithfulness, as borne out by the Marines' motto, *simper fidelis.* In olden times, for the Spartans, the Samurai, the medieval knights, loyalty was a pledge of fealty. This reminds us that loyalty involves trust. Loyalty is therefore allegiance to the Republic, obedience to orders, as well as personal and unit discipline. And as a sacred bond, loyalty involves a love of the brotherhood, and serves faithfully, even when it's not appreciated. Loyalty is the virtue that links one warrior to another.

For my part, loyalty is a noble expression that stems from that "communal experience" that warriors feel that they belong together. In his book, *The Warriors,* author Jesse Glenn Gray describes this sentiment:

The cause that calls comradeship into being may be the defense of one's country, the propagation of the one true religious faith, or a passionate political ideology; it may be the maintenance of honor or the recovery of a Helen of Troy. So long as there is a cause, the hoped-for objective may be relatively unimportant in itself. Through military reverses or the fatiguing and often horrible experiences of combat, the original purpose becomes obscured, the fighter is often sustained solely by the determination not to let down his comrades.

Numberless soldiers have died, more or less willingly not for country or honor or religious faith or for any other abstract good, but because they realized that by fleeing their post and rescuing themselves, they would expose their companions to greater danger. Such a loyalty to the group is the essence of fighting morale. The commander who can preserve and strengthen it knows that all other psychological or physical factors are little in comparison. The feeling of loyalty, it is clear, is the result, and not the cause, of comradeship.

In most of us there is a genuine longing for community with our human species, and at the same time an awkwardness and helplessness about finding the way to achieve it. Some extreme experience – mortal danger for the threat of destruction – is necessary to bring us fully together with our comrades or with nature. Comradeship reaches its peak in battle.

Men are true comrades only when each is ready to give up his life for the other, without reflection and without thought of personal loss. Such sacrifice seems hard and heroic to those who have never felt communal ecstasy. Nothing is further from the truth then the insistence of certain existentialist philosophers that each person must die his own death and experience it unsharably. If that were so, how many lives would have been spared on the battlefield! But in fact, death for men united with each other can be shared as few other of life's great moments can be. To be sure, it is not death as we know it usually in civilian life. In the German language men never die in battle. They fall. The term is exact for the expression of self-sacrifice when it is motivated by the feeling of comradeship I may fall, but I do not die, for that which is real for me goes forward and lives on in the comrades for whom I gave up my physical life.[2]

The brotherhood of arms has been described in similar ways since recorded history. Stephen Crane's classic, *The Red Badge of Courage,* takes place during the Civil War and centers on the experiences of Union Army Private, Henry Fleming. The following describes the young man's first engagement, and his sense of loyalty to his regiment:

He suddenly lost concern for himself and forgot to look at a menacing fate. He became not a man but a member. He felt that something of which he was a part – a regiment, an army, a cause, or a country – was in a crisis. He was welded into a common personality which was dominated by a single desire. For some moments he could not flee any more than a little finger can commit a revolution from a hand. If he had thought the regiment was about to be annihilated. Perhaps he could have amputated himself from it. But its noise gave him assurance. The regiment was like a firework that, once ignited, proceeds superior to circumstances until its blazing vitality fades. It wheezed and banged with a mighty power. He pictured the ground before it as strewn with the discomfited. There was a consciousness always of the presence of his comrades about him. He felt the subtle battle brotherhood more potent even than the cause for which they were fighting. It was a mysterious fraternity born of the smoke and danger of death.[3]

---

[2] J. Glenn Gray, *The Warriors: Reflections on Men in Battle* (New York: Bison, 1970), 40.
[3] Stephen Crane, *The Red Badge of Courage* (New York: Dover, 1990), 25.

The Behavior of Loyalty

Loyalty involves living for something greater than yourself. There was once a brave young man with a promising future, who had every prospect for a happy and fulfilling life. Twenty-one-year-old Nathan Hale was a captain in the Continental Army. Son of a Congregational church deacon from Coventry, Connecticut, he volunteered for a dangerous intelligence gathering mission in British occupied New York. The year was 1776. Washington's Army had been hounded out of the strategically vital port city. Hale's mission was to infiltrate New York and gain the enemy's disposition and defensive strength.

Dressed as a Dutch farmer, Hale infiltrated the British occupied city. Taking notes in Latin, he went through the entire British encampment, estimating their numbers and sketching their fortifications. Having obtained a trove of data, on his way back to the safety of American lines he was captured. Finding the notes in his boot, Hale was arrested for spying and told he would hang in the morning. He asked for a chaplain and a Bible, but both requests were denied. On the next morning, Hale wrote a few letters and prepared to die. At the scaffold, he spoke briefly, urging the spectators to be prepared to die at any moment. In the great spirit of loyalty, on the polar opposite of Benedict Arnold, Hale's last words before the rope swung him into eternity were, "I only regret that I have but one life to lose for my country." These are the words of one who uses his death as a means of proving his love and devotion to something greater than himself.

Chapter 4: Loyalty

Hale's death dignified his sacrifice. As I see him, Hale was triumphant in death. For those like him, dying in this sense is not a loss, but a gain.

A young Army officer, named James Nick Rowe, was imprisoned by the Viet Cong for five years until he escaped to freedom. The hell he endured for five years challenged his loyalties to his Country. In his book Five Years to Freedom, he writes,

The strong conflict in my mind between what I believed to be right and what Mafia (one of his Viet Cong captors) was striving to prove to me was right was a complication in the already serious confusion which existed. I knew what was expected of me as an officer; the loyalty and devotion to country and duty that an officer must exemplify, the faith and trust in our government and our cause, the belief in the support of the American people, for whom I believed we were fighting, and the ultimate good which would be wrought by our efforts, no matter how unclear the picture at the present time...The fear of immediate death was stilled, but the unknown was a greater burden. I couldn't imagine myself holding out for an extended period of time on the diet of rice and minute amounts of fish—when we had any at all. The hope for release was my source of strength.[4]

Nick Rowe is among America's great heroes for a few simple reasons. He pined away for five years in a bamboo cage, with a body wracked with pain and disease, but he never lost his faith in God or his hope in America. Suffering silently, he bided his time, waiting for the

---

[4] James N. Rowe, *Five Years to Freedom* (New York: Ballantine Books, 1971), 74.

opportunity to achieve his freedom. Never once did he betray his God or his country. Following five years in an earthly hell, Rowe returned home with honor. Added to this, unwilling to bury his trauma, he rather unearthed it, sharing his experiences, and created the Army's Survival, Evasion, Resistance and Escape (SERE) course.

Roy Benavidez

As a virtue, loyalty is essentially the honor of having your fellow countrymen depend on you. The word "loyalty" invokes powerful expressions of patriotism. It's a sacred bond that unites warriors, animating them, and energizing actions. Martin Luther once observed, "Where the battle rages, there the loyalty of the soldier is proved." This expression sums the actions of Master Sergeant Roy P. Benavidez.

It was a clear morning on 2 May 1968. A 12-man Special Forces team was being inserted by helicopters into the dense jungle west of Loc Ninh, Vietnam. A few miles away, Benavidez sat in a Forward Operating Base (FOB) monitoring the progress of the mission. The 5th Special Forces Group team was out gathering intelligence to confirm suspected large-scale enemy activity. The area of the team's insertion was routinely patrolled by the North Vietnamese Army (NVA). The helos had scarcely lifted off when the team met heavy enemy resistance and requested emergency extraction. Three helicopters braved the attempt but were driven off by intense enemy small arms and anti-aircraft fire.

Chapter 4: Loyalty

Incensed by the enemy's ferocity, and moved by his comrades' call for help, Benavidez boarded a returning aircraft to assist in yet another extraction attempt. Realizing that all the team members were either dead or wounded and unable to move to the pickup zone (PZ), Benavidez directed the aircraft to a nearby clearing. He jumped from the hovering helicopter and ran into what was soon to become hell's half-acre. From the field where he landed, he ran to the crippled team through the gauntlet of what amounted to one hundred and fifty feet under withering small arms fire. On the way there, he was wounded in his right leg, face, and head.

Despite these painful injuries, he took charge, repositioning the team members and directing their fire to facilitate the landing of an extraction aircraft, and the loading of wounded and dead team members. He then threw smoke canisters to direct the aircraft to the team's position. Despite his severe wounds and under intense enemy fire, he carried and dragged half of the wounded team members to the awaiting aircraft. He then provided protective fire by running alongside the aircraft as it moved to pick up the remaining team members.

As the enemy's fire intensified, he hurried to recover the body and classified documents on the dead team leader. When he reached the leader's body, he was severely wounded by small arms fire in the abdomen and received some grenade fragments in his back. At nearly the same moment, the aircraft pilot was mortally wounded, and his helicopter crashed. Although in extremely critical condition due to his multiple wounds,

Benavidez secured the classified documents and made his way back to the wreckage, where he aided the wounded out of the overturned aircraft and gathered the stunned survivors into a defensive perimeter.

Under increasing enemy automatic weapons and grenade fire, he moved around the perimeter distributing water and ammunition, re-instilling in the men a will to live and fight. Facing a buildup of enemy opposition with a beleaguered team, Benavidez began calling in tactical air strikes, directing the fire from supporting gunships to suppress the enemy and so permit another extraction attempt. He was wounded again in his thigh by small arms fire while administering first aid to a wounded team member just before another extraction helicopter was able to land.

His indomitable spirit kept him going as he began to ferry his comrades to the craft. On his second trip with the wounded, he was clubbed and suffered additional wounds to his head and arms before killing his adversary. He then continued under devastating fire to carry the wounded to the helicopter. Upon reaching the aircraft, he spotted and killed two enemy soldiers who were rushing the craft from an angle that prevented the aircraft door gunner from firing upon them.

With little strength remaining, he made one last trip to the perimeter to ensure that all classified material had been collected or destroyed, and to bring in the remaining wounded. Only then, in extremely serious condition from numerous wounds and loss of blood, did he allow himself to be pulled into the extraction aircraft. Sergeant Benavidez' gallant choice to join voluntarily his comrades who were in critical straits, to expose himself constantly to withering enemy fire, and his refusal to be stopped despite numerous severe wounds, saved the lives of at least eight men. His fearless personal leadership, tenacious devotion to duty, and extremely valorous actions in the face of overwhelming odds were in keeping with the highest traditions of the military service and reflect the utmost credit on him and the United States Army. Master Sergeant Roy Benavidez endured battle fatigue and hardship for the sake of those he fought to save. These are the finest qualities in a warrior.

The Balance of Loyalty

As with all the virtues, loyalty to others in the fraternity of arms must be balanced. In the words of Winston Churchill, "It is the fault of all booms of sentiment that they carry men too far and lead to reactions. Militarism degenerates into brutality. Loyalty promotes tyranny and sycophancy." Certainly, a pitfall and imbalance to avoid is becoming a lackey, or "yes man." We've all met this type. He's the suck up who'll say almost anything to win approval. The truth is people see right through such insincere activity. The point is unquestioning compliance is not loyalty. It is our duty to have an ongoing assessment of our loyalties.

Dienekes was a Spartan soldier, the bravest of all the Greeks, who fought and died at the Battle of Thermopylae in 480 BC. Preparing for the battle, Dienekes instructed his comrades:

Here is what you do, friends. Forget country. Forget king. Forget wife and children and freedom. Forget every concept, however noble, that you imagine you fight for here today. Act for this alone: for the man who stands at your shoulder. He is everything, and everything is contained within him. That is all I know. That is all I can tell you.[5]

Perhaps Mark Twain put it best when he said, "Loyalty to the country always. Loyalty to the government when it deserves it."

The Bond of Loyalty

This is perhaps best illustrated by the motto of the United States Marine Corps – *Semper Fidelis* – Latin for "always faithful" or "always loyal." Semper Fidelis is the motto of every Marine. In hundreds of battlefields, from the Mekong Delta to the sands of Iraq, these words have been shared among fellow Marines in their commitment to our Nation and its success. The words "Semper Fi" have rung true down through the centuries, distinguishing the Corps and emboldening Marines to do extraordinary deeds.

On the eve of the invasion of Iraq, Marine Corps General James Mattis addressed the 1st Reconnaissance Battalion Marines at Camp Pendleton:

---

[5] Steven Pressfield, *Gates of Fire: An Epic Novel of the Battle of Thermopylae* (New York: Bantam, 1999), 405.

Chapter 4: Loyalty

For decades, Saddam Hussein has tortured, imprisoned, raped and murdered the Iraqi people; invaded neighboring countries without provocation; and threatened the world with weapons of mass destruction. The time has come to end his reign of terror. On your young shoulders rest the hopes of mankind. When I give you the word, together we will cross the Line of Departure, close with those forces that choose to fight, and destroy them. Our fight is not with the Iraqi people, nor is it with members of the Iraqi army who choose to surrender. While we will move swiftly and aggressively against those who resist, we will treat all others with decency, demonstrating chivalry and soldierly compassion for people who have endured a lifetime under Saddam's oppression. Chemical attack, treachery, and use of the innocent as human shields can be expected, as can other unethical tactics. Take it all in stride.

Be the hunter, not the hunted: never allow your unit to be caught with its guard down. Use good judgment and act in best interests of our Nation. You are part of the world's most feared and trusted force. Engage your brain before you engage your weapon. Share your courage with each other as we enter the uncertain terrain north of the Line of Departure. Keep faith in your comrades on your left and right and Marine Air overhead. Fight with a happy heart and strong spirit. For the mission's sake, our country's sake, and the sake of the men who carried the Division's colors in the past battles-who fought for life and never lost their nerve, carry out your mission and keep your honor clean. Demonstrate to the world there is "No Better Friend, No Worse Enemy" than a U.S. Marine.[6]

To say the bond of loyalty is like saying the loyalty of loyalty. As illuminated by these words, honor is sacred,

---

[6] Nathaniel Fick, *One Bullet Away: The Making of a Marine Officer* (Boston: Mariner Books, 2005), 163.

and loyalty is the sacred bond that binds warriors together. Loyalty is therefore the backbone of a fighting force.

On November 21, 2010, twenty-year-old Lance Corporal Kyle Carpenter and a fellow Marine were standing guard on a roof in the village of Marjah, Helmand Province, Afghanistan. Their unit, Fox Company, 2nd Battalion, 9th Marine Regiment, was taking the fight to the Taliban. As the two Marines were nearing the end of their guard shift, Taliban fighters swarmed the village, and threw a hand grenade on the roof where they were.

Without hesitating, Lance Corporal Carpenter threw himself in front of the grenade to protect his fellow Marine. Carpenter recounts that within a few seconds he went unconscious believing he would forever leave this earth. Carpenter woke up five weeks later in Walter Reed Hospital. Large portions of his face, head, and right arm had been destroyed, requiring reconstructive surgery. A three-year process. Lance Corporal Kyle Carpenter's self-sacrificial actions that day in Helmand province epitomize the Marine Corps motto "Simper Fi."

Principles of Loyalty

It's the imperative of loyalty that dictates to warriors what to know and what to do. Again, two principles:

Know: <u>Duty is the privilege of service</u>. Understanding this is helpful when our loyal service is not appreciated.

Do: <u>Serve faithfully, even when it's not appreciated</u>. Loyalty is living for something greater than yourself. This is an effective check to the pride of vainglory, which is being mad with love for personal honor.

During the Second World War, the Japanese built Burma-Siam Railway. Spanning some 260 miles between Burma (now Myanmar) and Siam (now Thailand), the Japanese pressed thousands of POWs into service to complete the formidable task in under three years. Ernest Gordon was a Scottish POW who labored in this enterprise, experiencing hell on earth at the hands of his Japanese captors. Laboring under oppressive jungle heat, and fighting off disease and insects, it has been estimated that nearly 400 POWs died for every mile of track laid. Those unable to go on were beheaded or bayonetted to death. Describing the conditions these POWs faced, Ernest Gordon writes:

As conditions steadily worsened, as starvation, exhaustion and disease took an ever-growing toll, the atmosphere in which we lived was increasingly poisoned by selfishness, hatred, and fear. We were slipping rapidly down the scale of degradation. We lived by the rule of the jungle; survival of the fittest. It was a case of "I look out for myself and to hell with everyone else." The weak were trampled underfoot, the sick ignored or resented, the dead forgotten. When a man lay dying, we had no word of mercy. When he cried for our help, we averted our heads. We had long since resigned ourselves to being derelicts. We were forsaken men, and now, even God had left us. Hate, for some, was the only motivation for living. We hated the Japanese. We would willingly have torn them limb from limb, flesh from flesh, had they fallen into our hands.[1]

Then one day, a shovel changed everything. At the end of each day, Japanese guards would collect the tools from the work party. With the workday at an end, the tools were being counted. But as the work party was to be dismissed, a Japanese guard shouted that a shovel was missing. In a fury he demanded the guilty man to step forward to take his punishment. No one moved. "All die! All die!" he shrieked, cocking and aiming his rifle at the

---

[1] Ernest Gordon, *The Miracle on the River Kwai* (Berkeley, CA: Collins, 1963), 87.

prisoners. As he was about to fire, one man stepped forward. The guard beat him with his fists while the man stood silently at attention. Then in a rage, the guard clubbed the man to death with his rifle. When they returned to the camp, the tools were counted again, and no shovel was missing.[2]

Word spread like wildfire through the whole camp. An innocent man had been willing to die to save others. This one man's selfless sacrifice revolutionized the camp's atmosphere, and the POWs began to treat each other like brothers again. "Greater love has no one than this, than to lay down one's life for his friends" (John 15:13).

---

[2] Ibid., 117.

Introspection

I have purposely bookended each chapter with five introspective questions. These are designed to promote professional growth:

1. What order of precedence do you place the following: God, family, Country?

2. Can you serve faithfully even when your service is unappreciated?

3. Can you consider that others are more important than yourself?

4. Can you serve faithfully even if no one notices?

5. How important is the brotherhood of arms?

Washington rallies the troops at the Battle of Monmouth, June 28, 1778.

5

Temperance

"Most powerful is he who has himself in his own power."
— Seneca

While it may be said that temperance is arguably the least talked about virtue, it is the one most evident when its lacking. For instance, youthful intemperance leads many a troop to overindulge. On the other hand, however, it's temperance that holds all the virtues together. Now, some may find it strange to have temperance considered as a warrior virtue. Aren't warriors called to surge forth in fury upon their foes? After all, the greatest of war epics, Homer's *Iliad*, is arguably about warrior anger. However, as readily observed in that ancient poem, such intemperance in warriors leads to unnecessary and unhealthy extremes.

Growing up, I loved the *Iliad*, and idolized the epic warrior Achilles. Superficially, every boy wants to be him. It's easy to be seduced by his demigod power, and lion-like courage. Albeit, in the pages of Homer's epic, Achilles' rage goes unchecked and is highly destructive; not merely to the enemy Trojans mind you. His inability to control himself leads him to commit various acts of sacrilege, particularly in the desecration of Hector's body after killing him. In the last analysis, it may be said that Achilles' strength, warrior prowess, and skill masked his critical deficiency of temperance.

America is great because she is good. One of the things that makes America great is that while we prosecute wars that can have devastating effects on our enemies, we do so with restraint. That is, while dealing out death, we limit collateral damage and prevent the unnecessary use of force. As a military, our collective intelligence and temperance exercises great influence on the way we conduct war. With such collective values, the US military disdains any such action as those of Achilles save lion-like courage.

Definition

Temperance is moderation or voluntary self-restraint in thought, feeling or action. In the Greek, temperance, *sophrosune*, is also a Stoic cardinal virtue. As such, any discussion on this virtue uncovers a trove of Stoic gems. As defined by Cicero, temperance is "domination of reason over desire and over other incorrect inclinations of the mind." By this definition, temperance includes everything from sex to nutrition. In his *Meditations*, the Stoic philosopher Emperor Marcus Aurelius defined temperance as "a virtue opposed to love of pleasure." As is commonly known, the Stoics see emotion as potentially highly destructive. Emotional signals can be misread leading us to excesses. The thing is, emotions cannot be removed from our lives. However, as the Stoics would counsel us, we can repurpose their potentially destructive power.

Considering again, the famous rage of Achilles, many see the epic hero and assent to his anger as an acceptable emotion in war. As such, anger is not normally viewed as a weakness. For the Stoics, it is. As noted by Nancy Sherman,

Stoicism regards anger as a sign of vulnerability in the same way that grief or fear is, for we experience each when we allow ourselves to become invested in things that are outside our own control. The angry person reacts to affronts to honor or respect, the grieving person to loss, and the fearful person to danger in a way that the Stoics argue threatens the self-sufficiency necessary for good living. Indeed, anger, in a way more obvious than fear or grief, reveals a defensive (and at times retributivist) posture that at its rawest often seems just an impulse to bite back at those who bit us.[1]

---

[1] Nancy Sherman, *Stoic Warriors: The Ancient Philosophy Behind the Military Mind* (New York: Oxford, 2005), 65.

It is worth noting that according to the Stoics, a desire for honor is likewise an external investment, which lies outside our control, which, if we wrongly invest in, can have equally destructive fallouts.

In his book *Meditations*, Marcus Aurelius countlessly reminded himself not to be impulsive. Here are a few quotes:

"Stop letting your emotions override what your mind tells you." Meditations 2.2

"Stop letting yourself be pulled in all directions." 2.7

"Never act out of compulsion." 3.5

As Marcus Aurelius would agree, temperance separates humans from mere animals. By reason we understand the appetites, rather than be used by them. How this pertains to soldiering was perhaps put best by Alexander the Great. Realizing that a nation's survival depends on its warrior class, he said, "The end and perfection of our victories is to avoid the vices and infirmities of those whom we subdue."

The Vikings agree: "Rage blinds truth."[2]

The Character of Temperance

According to Cicero, temperance "maintains the well-weighed judgments of the mind." For the ancients, this virtue gave a sort of polish to life, which the Romans

---

[2] Fóstbrœðra Saga, Chapter 22.

referred to as decorum. There are four cardinal virtues in the ancient philosophical system known as Stoicism. These are prudence (practical wisdom), justice, fortitude (courage), and temperance. Regarding temperance, Cicero noted that its aspects include "orderliness of conduct and opportuneness of times." As Cicero would have it, "we must also follow the established customs and conventions of the community in which we find ourselves." With this in mind, temperance calls for one to act and speak in a sense of moderation that befits the occasion. In other words, temperance is "doing the right thing at the right time." As such, temperance is the science of self-control.

Temperance is a rational harness to impulse. It is self-mastery. A lack of temperance is obvious when its lacking. The Stoic philosopher Cleanthes once described how intemperance looks. He said a man who allows himself to be led around by his emotions is likened to a dog tied to a cart that is compelled to go wherever the cart (of emotion) leads on. Cleanthes' adage underscores the necessity of temperance. That is, if we desire to live well. Maintaining emotional balance is indeed a challenge.

The Dichotomy of Control

Some of the most useful Stoic teachings are derived from a work entitled *The Enchiridion*. Based on the teachings of Epictetus, this work is a small, handy collection of the most directly applicable teachings of Stoicism. The work begins with the thought:

There are things which are within our power, and there are things which are beyond our power. Within our power are opinion, aim, desire, aversion, and, in one word, whatever affairs are our own. Beyond our power are body, property, reputation, office, and, in one word, whatever are not properly our own affairs.

This principle Stoic tenet is what is commonly called the "Dichotomy of Control." Why this is important should be easily seen. The goal of Stoicism is to develop the mind to such an extent that the practitioner reaches a state of being called *eudaimonia*, which is the state of happiness that comes from living well. Eudaimonia literally means "good spirit." Wanting to have control over things in life but finding them outside your grasp can lead one to become frustrated and anxious.

Stoicism is the art of living well. In order to live well, you must differentiate between things that are worth fretting about and things that are not worth fretting about (Well, more like things to concern yourself with and not fret). The obvious benefits from this freeing construct cannot be overstated. If you adopt this mindset, you will feel truly liberated.

Precisely what things are "within our power?" To begin with, our judgment about things, including both our desires and our emotions. This is in fact the ground floor of Viktor Frankl's therapeutic modality he developed in Auschwitz. According to his Logotherapy, forces beyond our control can take everything away from us "except our freedom to choose the manner in which we will respond to the situation."[3] Frankl was unconsciously (or consciously?) echoing Epictetus, "Men are disturbed not by things, but by the views which they take of them."

Things beyond our control include our body. To be sure, we can eat less and lose weight or lift weights and gain muscle, but we cannot control our genetics or our predisposition to illness. We also may not have control over property or possessions. These may be stolen. Perhaps closest to home for warriors, more than likely, we cannot control where we deploy, and we certainly cannot control someone's opinion of us.

Regarding the latter, Epictetus once remarked, "If anyone tells you that a certain person speaks ill of you, do not make excuses about what is said of you, but answer: "He was ignorant of my other faults, else he would not have mentioned these alone."[4] With so much beyond our control, we need concern ourselves with only one thing: our own judgments, emotions, and actions. This is the only power we have, but the only power we really need.

For a Stoic, outcome is nothing, action that is under control is everything. The oft-quoted prayer of Reinhold Niebuhr reflects this: "God grant me the serenity to accept the things I cannot change; courage to change the things I can; and wisdom to know the difference."

---

[3] Viktor Frankl, *Man's Search for Meaning* (Boston: Beacon Press, 2006), 66.
[4] *Enchiridion*, XXXIII.

Viking 26

The following is a story related by Sergeant Major Adam Thompson:

"Ok bros, you know the drill, around the room." The room is the war room. The room where Viking 26 conducted Pre-combat checks (PCCs), before every mission. The room every man turned to his left and right and checked, checked, and re-checked his brother to make sure he had everything he needed for a 24-hour dismounted operation in eastern Afghanistan. The room were the team kept their kit. The room where they ate their meals together. The room in which they planned together and where they prepared one last time to step on the devil's dance floor. "We're up boss. Check's complete." You could hear as the helicopters inbound to fly us again into a 24-hour direct-action clearance operation. I gaze around one more time in the room. They're ready; they were always ready. "Ok bros, bow your heads."

I take a deep breath and pause for a second. We lock arms, then recite the battle hymn, "We stand at the ready for the cowards to come, the canyons will rattle at the sound of our guns. No mercy, no quarter, they'll pay for their sins, now lower the cannons, the battle begins! Ok boys let's go to work." This was the battle cry of Viking 26 in the fighting season of 2013 in eastern Afghanistan.

Like most Operational Detachment Alphas (ODAs), or Green Berets, teams ebb and flow. Peaks and valleys as we would say. Sometimes teams will be in a funk with a bad Team Sergeant, bad Team Leader, or just a team with a bad attitude. Such teams didn't fly under the radar. For the most part, after almost ten years of conflict, teams were solid. Most teams had a few "grey beards" with multiple combat tours who could help the new jacks on the team get up to speed.

In the fall of 2012, Viking 26 was hitting on all cylinders. Tons of experience. Lots of combat rotations, and an experienced Team Sergeant. Eventually they got a solid Team Leader and put it all together. The boys trained hard, real hard. Close Quarters Combat (CQC), Tactical Combat Casualty Care (TCCC), Close air support (CAS), and learning each other's jobs inside and out. Also, and most importantly, the team was close, very close. They trusted each other, counted on each other, and knew they could always, always count on each other. And to this day, they are still best friends. Paired with the Sixth Special Operations Kandak (6th SOK), or Afghan Commando's, the team would conduct raids throughout the spring, summer and fall of 2013.

I remember thinking before every mission, the most important thing to me was bringing the boy's home. I owed that to them. I owed that to their families. And the best way I saw to meet that intent, was to be fast, swift, and be violent, really violent. For me it was momentum. As soon as we land, win the battlefield; breach, shoot and continue to move. If we were moving and dominating space, we would be ok. It was all about aggression. I remember hearing teams on the radio calling in saying they were "troops in contact" (TIC), stating, "we are taking effective fire, permission to engage with organic weapons systems?"

I remember thinking, "Permission to shoot back? What the hell's wrong with you? Grab your sack and get after it. Close the distance and dominate. How the hell did you let your team get in that position in the first place?" Never made sense to me. You are in a gun fight, be violent! Hindsight being 2020, maybe the rules of engagement (ROE) had some of these young officers scared. Not scared of the enemy, scared to get fired. Scared of losing their career. Shame on anyone who put them in this situation, looking out for their career. Toxic leadership. Anyway, this was not the case on my team, nor did I care about being fired. I was in the business of my boys surviving, through violent and kinetic means. And truth be told, no team did it better. By the time the summer had drawn to a close, we had cleared and held most of the valleys in Wardak, Logar, and Kapisa. We never lost a single US soldier on the battlefield and killed more than 150 enemy combatants. But some things you just can't train for.

The morning of September 21, 2013 started like most mornings. The Team Leader and I had gone up to the Commando compound to speak with the partner force about the next mission. The boys were just north of us on the range, training the Commandos in basic rifle marksmanship. We left the compound and pulled back into our Fire base, just down the road. As we hopped off our four wheelers, the front gate burst open with one of the Commando's coyote tan trucks. The first guy out of the vehicle was an interpreter screaming and one of our medics were bleeding from the face. I yelled for our medics and immediately my Team Leader called for a medical evacuation via helicopter (MEDEVAC). As our medics began working on him, I was amazed that he was still able to talk. As he recounted, a grenade went off in the truck he was in. Glass covered his face. You could also clearly see he had two bullet wounds to the face. The Afghan interpreter was so hysterical he couldn't talk.

I told my boys, who were already grabbing their kit and loading up, to "get up to the range and tell me what the hell was going on." I relayed the status of the patient to my Team Leader. This way, when the medevac landed, they would know how to treat the patient. A few minutes went by. Then, one of my guys called on the radio, "hey boss, we have three dead US up here on the range." As he relayed their battle roster numbers my heart sank. We had just had a green on blue. A member of our partner force had turned on us. The one thing you never think will happen to you. Suffice it to say, the experience and wisdom of my team astonished me. They were not trained for this. This is not something you sit around in the shoot house or on the range and talk about "so, how do we prevent a green on blue, or an insider attack?" This was out of nowhere.

Our partner force was just terrified on how we would retaliate, they felt we would think they were to blame, that they should have known. But we knew that was not the case. But that was precisely what the Taliban wanted, to drive a wedge in our commitment to each other. To forge a wedge between two partners with different languages and different cultures fighting under one common goal. To liberate the oppressed. To secure a future for the people of Afghanistan. This tactic the Taliban practiced certainly ruin units, destroying the bonds units worked to foster over years of conflict. That was not the case with us.

After we put our fallen on the helicopters, my team, against the wishes of our Commanders, went up to the partner force compound without weapons or body armor where we found them terrified and confused, and honestly waiting for us to kill them. As Green Berets we are taught to be smarter, lead with tenacity and compassion, and have the emotional intelligence to make the right decisions. We assured them our bonds are still strong, and they could have no idea about the insider threat. The Afghan Commander and Sergeant Major insisted they fly to BAF to honor our fallen. And that is what they did. They both shed tears at the ramp side ceremony sending our hero's home.

I think about this almost daily, about our three warriors who fought hard not only in the summer of 2013, but most of their adult lives. I think about the sacrifice they made, the sacrifice their families made. I think about things I could have done differently; I think about how we could have prepared better. And then I remember what one of my boys said to me "Some things you just cannot train for." It would be easy for me to tell you about all the epic gunfights and battles we got into the summer of 2013, and if I did, it would be only to tell you how proud and humbled I am to have shared the same dirt with the

Vikings of 26. I share this to keep you aware, keep you sharp, and keep your mind prepared for anything. And if that time comes, and I hope it does not, take that tactical pause. Breathe.

L.N., J.S., T.M., till we meet again brothers. You live within us every day. To the boys of 26, 24, 1220, you know who you are. "Fara i Viking." As Magnus, the last Northman king to fall in battle said, "It is good to end a stout life with a stout death."[5]

The Challenge of Temperance

Doing what we feel comes easy, restraining an urge is often not. In Aristotle's book, *Rhetoric*, observing various faults of character, he notes:

The causes of our deliberately intending harmful and wicked acts contrary to law are (1) vice, and (2) lack of self-control. For the wrongs of man does to others who will correspond to the bad quality or qualities that he himself possesses. Thus, it is the mean man who will wrong others about money, the profligate and matters of physical pleasure, the effeminate and matters of comfort, and the coward were danger is concerned- his terror makes him abandon those who are involved in the same danger. The ambitious man does wrong for the sake of honor, the quick tempered from anger, the lover of victory for the sake of victory, the embittered man for the sake of revenge, the stupid man because he has misguided notions of right and wrong, the shameless man because he does not mind what people think of him; And so with the rest – any wrong that

---

[5] *The Saga of Magnus Barefoot*, Chapter 6.

anyone does to others corresponds to his particular faults of character.[6]

There is a sinister variety of delight known to veterans regarding the destruction of the enemy. Holding our enemy's lives in contempt, there is a certain gleeful joy associated with their demise. As author Jesse Glenn Gray puts it, "Men who have lived in the zone of combat long enough to be veterans or sometimes possessed by a fury that makes them capable of anything. Blinded by the rage to destroy and supremely careless of consequences, they storm against the enemy until they are either victorious, dead, or utterly exhausted. It is as if they are seized by a demon and are no longer in control of themselves. From the Homeric account of the sacking of Troy to the conquest of Dien Bien Phu, Western literature is filled with descriptions of soldiers as berserkers and mad destroyers."[7]

As a member of America's most elite fighting units, I was privileged to take part in the wars in Iraq and Afghanistan. On one such raid, my unit came upon some Al Qaeda. Certain AQI fighters had managed to badly injure some team guys. Like avenging angels, the unit team surreptitiously entered a compound and stood poised over some terrorists lying in a room. When they opened up on those guys, you could literally feel the hatred they had for them. Holding their lives in contempt, they slaughtered them to the man. As the one-way

---

[6] Aristotle, *Rhetoric*, 10.20.
[7] J. Glenn Gray, *The Warriors: Reflections on Men in Battle* (New York: Bison, 1970), 51.

gunfight went on in the room, and the number of bullets began to mount, the kill or capture mission turned into one of blood lust. Due to the high volume of bullets whizzing around the room, one of them ricocheted off the wall and hit a teammate in the leg. The incident went from saving our teammate's leg to saving his life.

This episode reminded me that chivalric temperance manages violence, and that the weapons of war are not to be used for vindictiveness. In the section of his book regarding ethics in war, theologian John Murray once noted:

The sword is never intrinsically, and should never be practically, the instrument of vengeance and malicious hate. Whenever a nation, and especially a soldier on the field of battle, uses weapons of war as instruments of vindictive revenge rather than instruments of retributive justice than the dictates of both justice and love have been desecrated.[8]

As General Sherman once noted, "war is hell." War is a crucible in which the metal of our character is tested. It brings out the best and worst in everyone. Hating one's enemies comes naturally. The profession of arms however calls for warriors to not hate those in front of them but rather love those with them, and behind them.

---

[8] John Murray, *Principles of Conduct: Aspects of Biblical Ethics*, 179.

The Compensation of Temperance

Like integrity, a lack of temperance in a Soldier, Sailor, Marine, or Airmen can be the greatest contributor to personal unhappiness. In light of that, to say that temperance pays great dividends is an understatement. Taking stock of my younger life, I consider the pain and misfortune I could have avoided if only I could have controlled myself.

Temperance is mastery over instincts and keeps desires within the limits of what is deemed honorable. The military is famous for its acronyms. These are used because acronyms help us memorize things. Perhaps the Stoic's greatest stock in trade was their emphasis on emotional regulation. In light of that, here's an acronym I developed to help keep myself in check: **STOIC**

S – <u>Stay in the Present</u>. Imagination has its place. Stay focused. For Marcus Aurelius, nothing was more pathetic than people who run around in circles.[9] For the present, as he reminds us, is of the same duration everywhere. "Though you were to live three thousand, or, if you please, thirty thousand of years, yet remember that no man can lose any other life than that which he now lives, neither is he possessed of any other than that which he loses. Whence it follows that the longest life, as we commonly speak, and the shortest, come all to the same reckoning." As such, "when the longest and shortest-lived persons come to die, their loss is equal; they can but lose the

---

[9] *Meditations* 2.13.

PRESENT as being the only thing they have; for that which he has not, no man can be truly said to lose."[10]

"Each of us lives only now, this brief instant. The rest has been lived already or is impossible to see. The span we live is small, small as the corner of the earth in which we live it."[11] Here and now, "it suffices to manage the present well."[12] "Be not disturbed about the future, for if ever you come to it, you will have the same reason for your guide, which preserves you at present."[13]

The point is, staying in the present helps you stay in reality. Thinking this way, frees us from other distractions. We are reminded that we suffer more in the imagination then we do in reality. This will help us avoid suffering imaginary troubles. Hence, stay in the present and stay in reality. The key word is "reality."

T – Think Critically. Take in the big picture. The goal is to get what I call the thirty-six-thousand-foot view. Such a view helps us to stay focused. To mix metaphors, we often can't see the forest for the trees. It's only when we step back a bit and widen our aperture that we see things more clearly. The challenge here is to see things as they really are. For Marcus Aurelius, "Reason and the reasoning faculty need no foreign assistance but are sufficient for their own purposes."[14] Thinking critically

---

[10] Ibid., 2.14.
[11] Ibid., 3.14.
[12] Ibid., 6.2.
[13] Ibid., 7.8.
[14] Ibid., 5.14.

helps us realize the big picture. The optimal word here is "<u>realize</u>."

O – <u>Optimize</u>. Because events can overwhelm us if we let them, we live our best life when we direct our energy toward what really matters. Concerning this, Epictetus opines, "If you ever happen to turn your attention to externals, for the pleasure of anyone, be assured that you have ruined your scheme of life."[15]

"Concentrate every minute like a Roman – like a man – on doing what's in front of you with precise and genuine seriousness, tenderly, willingly, with justice. Not freeing yourself from all other distractions. Yes, you can- if you do everything as if it were the last thing you were going to do in life, and stop being aimless, stop letting your emotions override what your mind tells you, stop being hypocritical, self-centered, irritable. You will see how few things you have to do to live a satisfying and reverent life. If you can manage this, that's all even the gods can ask of you."[16] Work toward manageable goals. The optimal word here is "<u>realistic</u>."

I – <u>Impulse-Control</u>. Control your emotions or they will control you. An adult male who cannot control his emotions calls into question his manhood. In fact, such a male could aptly be called an emotional infant. This reminds us to reset emotionally before we allow ourselves to become imbalanced. This quality is what psychologists call emotional intelligence (EI), the capacity to blend

---

[15] *Enchiridion*, XXIII.
[16] *Meditations* 2.5.

thinking and feeling to make optimal decisions. EI is one's capacity to be aware of and control one's emotions so as to handle interpersonal situations judiciously and empathetically.

For Aristotle, the best life was lived within the golden mean or middle way. In his *Nicomachean Ethics*, he discusses how imbalances are due to either excesses or defects:

For the man who flies from and fears everything and does not stand his ground against anything becomes a coward, and the man who fears nothing at all but goes to meet every danger becomes rash; and similarly the man who indulges in every pleasure and abstains from none becomes self-indulgent, while the man who shuns every pleasure, as bores do, becomes in a way insensible; temperance and courage, then, are destroyed by excess and defect, and preserved by the mean.[17]

According to psychologists, emotions are "chemicals that help us regulate our minds and bodies, assisting us to cope with the complexities of making decisions, interacting with people, and finding our way through life. Each burst of emotion chemicals, from the time its produced in the hypothalamus to the time it's completely broken down and absorbed, lasts about six seconds." A skill I've acquired, and I'm working to perfect (which will take the rest of my life), is the six second rule.

Here's how it's supposed to work. Someone cuts you off in traffic. Taking a six second pause as you hit your brakes or maneuver out of the way of this "genius" engages the

---

[17] Aristotle, *Nicomachean Ethics*, Book II, 2. 1104.

analytical part of your brain for at least six seconds. Experts determine this is the minimum amount of time needed to create an emotional interruption. During this six second of higher-order thinking, during which time you can simply count or enumerate six meaningful things, we can reset those feelings.

In *Meditations*, Marcus Aurelius constantly reminds himself about impulse control. "Do not suffer your passions to make a puppet of you. Confine your care to the present."[18] Now, the Stoics weren't perfect though they strove for it. Marcus Aurelius admitted to many mistakes. But he strove for excellence, reminding himself, "let your impulse always be under your control."[19] When mistakes were made, he reminded himself to "rouse and recollect yourself, and you will perceive your trouble lay only in a scene of imagination."[20] "What an easy matter it is to stem the current of your imagination, to discharge a troublesome or improper thought, <u>and at once return to a state of calm</u>."[21] The key word here is "<u>reset</u>."

C – <u>Commit to Excellence</u>. Lessons hard-earned can be easily forgotten. Don't throw away your learning. Temperance compensates us, paying us dividends. Go to school on yourself and apply the lessons learned. Life is a learning competition.

For the Stoics, reflecting on the day, as to what was good or bad was of immense importance. Journalling

---

[18] Ibid., 7. 29.
[19] Ibid., 12.17.
[20] Ibid., 6.31.
[21] Ibid., 5.2.

should be thought of in this way. Every night, Marcus Aurelius would write in his diary. He wrote to himself about daily challenges. He wrote about what he had learned throughout the day, including what he felt he had done well or not so well. His diary survived the test of time. We now recognize it as *The Meditations*. Reminding us of Stoic reflection, the key word here is "reflect."

Time Management

Perhaps a close second to controlling one's emotions is managing time. For most of us this is a challenge. William Penn once put it this way, "Time is what we want the most, but what we use the worst." Many waste time; loads of it. But once it's gone, it can never be recovered. You can get lost in a project or spend too much time watching tv or playing video games. A practice I recommend against. There's a song by Jim Croce that laments the fact that we cannot put *Time in a Bottle*. We either use it wisely or fritter it away foolishly.

Time management is the ability to plan and control how you spends the hours in a day to effectively accomplish your goals. This is an important aspect of temperance. I want to suggest four principles for the wise use of time (they also work for managing money). Use the acronym: **PART**

P – Prioritize tasks and define your goals. Establish clear goals and priorities in order to set aside non-essential tasks that can eat up time and to monitor where the time actually goes. This means saying "no" to some things. We have to do this.

In the film *Yes Man*, Jim Carrey's character Carl, is a bank loan officer that has a negative outlook on life. He's coaxed to attend a motivational seminar that encourages people to seize the opportunities life offers by saying "yes!" Carl is challenged to say "yes!" to every opportunity that presents itself. Throughout his many misadventures, Carl has to learn to say "no." Before, all he ever said was "no." In the film, Carl learns when to say "no," or better yet, he learned a better way is to say "yes," selectively. The point is, prioritizing involves being judicial. Sometimes what you don't do is as important as what you do. Be selective. Saying "no" to one thing enables you to say "yes" to other things.

Perhaps Marcus Aurelius put it best: "Most of what we say and do is unnecessary: remove the superfluity, and you will have more time and less bother. So, in every case one should prompt oneself: 'Is this, or is it not, something necessary?' And the removal of the unnecessary should apply not only to actions but to thoughts also: then no redundant actions either will follow."[22]

In their book, *The Warrior's Book of Virtues*, US Navy and Marine Corps veterans, Nick Benas, Matt Bloom, and Buzz Bryan, offer the following great advice:

Trim and slim down your activities. Say no to that committee, fundraiser, speaking engagement or request

---

[22] Marcus Aurelius, *Meditations* 4.24

for pet sitting unless it feeds you or gives you a sense of joy. Reduce the amount of escapist activities you partake in (social media, video games, and other mindless distractions).[23]

It's only when we stop trying to do everything and stop saying yes to everyone, that we can direct our energy to the few things that really matter to us, which are the essentials. Prioritize and use time for the true essentials and learn the power of "no." Use the mantra less but better. Less is more.

A – Adjust and reconfigure as needed. Don't be afraid of adjustment. Allow me to say a word on reflection. A helpful habit to keep ourselves and things in balance is journaling. Arguably, temperance is the most Stoic of all virtues.

As it is said, life is what happens when you're busy making other plans. We can be busy but non-productive. We often juggle things and over commit. Using personal calendars, journaling, and note-taking help eliminate non-essentials. This means we may have to make tradeoffs, as Kierkegaard once observed, "Life is not a problem to be solved, but a reality to be experienced."

R – Reserve time to think, recreate, and sleep. The central concept in Greg McKeown's book *Essentialism* is found in the subtitle, *The Disciplined Pursuit of Less*. There is in fact an undisciplined pursuit of more. In this

---

[23] Nick Benas, Matt Bloom, and Buzz Bryan, *The Warrior's Book of Virtues: A Field Manual for Living Your Best Life* (Hobart, NY: Hatherleigh Press, 2021), 41.

day and age, we can quickly become overwhelmed with a paralysis of analysis exhaustion stemming from the very legion of possibilities. It takes discipline to pursue less.

If there's one important physiological lesson the rigors of military service schools underscore it's the necessity of sleep to optimal performance. As a Special Forces instructor, I've seen guys get completely burned out and near worthless from lack of sleep. I recall running around in full kit, with loaded weapons and explosive charges, doing close quarters battle (CQB), and being dangerous. Dangerous because at that point I had been up for an extended amount of time and needed some sleep! Our instructors brought us to that point to not only see what we had as far as endurance goes, but to also show us how important sleep was (a lesson I already knew from the Ranger course). How much sleep is needed? Famously, Napoleon was one who needed a mere three or four hours a night. Most of us will need more. We all need to figure out what our needs are and make sure we account for it.

The point is it's extremely important that you allocate time to just unplug yourself from life. This may involve leaving your cellphone behind. Take up a hobby. Create margin for other activities beside work. Your mind and body need time for other activities. If there were such a thing as a 36-hour day, most of us would go none-stop, and reach tracer burnout. But that's when we become dangerous and make mistakes. The law of diminishing returns says there's only so much you can do cognitively and physically. This reminds us to form good habits to limit nonessentials.

T – <u>Timebox</u>. Timeboxing is a simple time management technique that involves allotting a fixed, maximum unit of time for any given activity. Timeboxing is all about having the forethought of setting aside time in advance, and then having the discipline of completing the activity within that time frame. This strategy necessitates only dedicating so much time to a given activity. When the time allotted is reached, an evaluation needs to be made. This will help us not to waste the precious commodity of time. After all, time is our most precious resource. As it is said: Time is free but its priceless. It cannot be owned, only spent. Spend your time wisely.

Looking back at these various aspects, the quality of temperance is seen in the man who is in control of his actions, how they affect others, and more importantly, how his actions influence the mission at hand. Temperance is being able to turn away from the temptations of temporary pleasure and immediate self-gratification.[24]

Let it be said that the maintaining of balance in life is king. Many extremes can be avoided by living within what Aristotle extolled as the golden mean.

---

[24] *The Warrior's Book of Virtues*, 45.

Principles of Temperance

Regarding temperance, here are two principles:

Know: <u>Temperance is mastery over instinct</u>. Understand it's not the events themselves that disturb us, rather it's our judgment of them.

Do: <u>Focus on what you can control</u>. We must control our emotions, or they will control us. This reminds us to put every impression, judgment call, and emotion, to the test before acting on it, above all, avoid making emotional decisions. This also reminds us that we may not be in control of what happens to us, but we can control how we respond to things.

Chapter 5: Temperance

Introspection

I have purposely bookended each chapter with five introspective questions. These are designed to promote professional growth:

1. Do you feel like you need more discipline in your life?

2. How you can you apply these principles to develop self-control?

3. Do you feel you are spending your time and resources wisely?

4. Have you had any instances when you lost your temper?

5. What did that occasion teach you?

Mad Anthony Wayne leading a bayonet charge
at Stony Point, July 16, 1779.

6

Courage

"I learned that courage was not the absence of fear, but the triumph over it. The brave man is not he who does not feel afraid, but he who conquers that fear." – Winston Churchill

It goes without saying that our chosen profession of arms is a dangerous one. Having such a dangerous line of work necessitates the need to deal with the very real possibility of death. Because war is the realm of danger, courage is the warrior's first requirement. In a sense, courage binds all the warrior virtues together. Courage is acting on one's own convictions despite the consequences. The virtue of courage involves both a physical and moral dimension.

Definition

In keeping with the Greek words that I have introduced for each virtue, courage is *tharsos,* and literally means stout-hearted. Courage may be defined as action despite the fear of death. It's the virtue of courage that enables a warrior to have, as it were, a perfect sensibility of danger, and a willingness to expose himself to it, nonetheless. Unlike the other virtues, courage is of two kinds. There is mental courage, the kind of courage in the face of personal danger. There is also moral courage. This is courage to accept responsibility.

Mental courage requires overcoming fears of bodily harm. This variety of courage involves taking risks in combat in spite of the fear of wounds or even death. As the US Marines understand it, fear is merely the human reaction to danger. "Everybody feels fear. Courage is not the absence of fear; rather, it is the strength to overcome fear."[1]

As to moral courage, this aspect of courage accepts responsibility, is doing one's duty despite a fear of

---

[1] U.S. Marine Corps, *Warfighting* MCDP 1-3 (Washington, D.C.: Government Printing Office, 2002), 9.

ostracism. Putting it all together, courage is essentially every virtue at its testing point.

Regarding physical courage, Clausewitz observes:

Combat gives rise to the element of danger in which all military activity must move and be maintained like birds in air and fish in water. The effects of danger, however, produce an emotional reaction, either as a matter of immediate instinct, or consciously. The former results in an effort to avoid the danger, or, where that is not possible, in fear and anxiety. Where these effects do not arise, it is because instinct has been outweighed by courage. But courage is by no means a conscious act; like fear, it is an emotion. Fear is concerned with physical and courage with moral survival. Courage is the nobler instinct, and as such cannot be treated as an inanimate instrument that functions simply as prescribed. So, courage is not simply a counterweight to danger, to be used for neutralizing its effects: it is a quality on its own.[2]

Mental Courage

The philosopher Montaigne once observed, "He who fears he will suffer, already suffers from his fear." This is essentially a paraphrase of the Stoic philosopher Zeno who likewise observed that fear is an expectation of evil. On the table of my memory, on which youth and observation have taken note of excellent phrases, one of my favorite expressions, is "you die before going into battle." While I believe this is a very good expression for warriors, its immediate worth is not readily

---

[2] Carl von Clausewitz, *On War*, Michael Howard and Peter Paret Translation (New York: Everyman's Library, 1993), Book II, Chapter 1, 138.

comprehended. The expression comes to us from the Japanese warrior philosophy called Bushido.

Encapsulating the essence of this thought, Inazo Nitobe observes, "For the Samurai, a sense of calm trust in Fate, a quiet submission to the inevitable, that stoic composure in sight of danger or calamity, became a kind of friendliness with death. And firmly resolved to an inevitable death, and hardening one's resolution to die in battle, the Samurai became as one already dead." Miyamoto Musashi, in his volume entitled *The Book of Five Rings* mirrors this by saying, "The way of the warrior is a resolute acceptance of death." Offering yet another echo of this same sentiment, in his book *Hagakure*, Yamamoto Tsunetomo observes, "If everyone were in accord and left things to Providence, their hearts would be at ease."

Articulating this virtue, in his book *Hagakure*, Yamamoto Tsunetomo outlines several crucial fundamentals. These include:

1. <u>There is nothing outside the thought of the immediate moment</u> (Hagakure, 30). Tsunetomo goes on to say, "There is surely nothing other than the single purpose of the present moment. A man's whole life is a succession of moment after moment. If one fully understands the present moment, there will be nothing else to do, and nothing else to pursue. Live being true to the single purpose of the moment. Everyone lets the present moment slip by, then looks for it as though he thought it were somewhere else. No one seems to have noticed this

fact. But grasping this firmly, one must pile experience upon experience. And once one has come to this understanding, he will be a different person from that point on, though he may not always bear it in mind."[3]

Recall the Stoics: stay in the present and stay in reality. Do as the situation deserves.

2. Live firmly resolved in your inevitable death (Hagakure 31). "Death is always at one's door."[4] "Death is the only sincerity. Becoming as a dead man in one's daily living is following the path of sincerity."[5] "Thus, the Way of the Samurai is, morning after morning, the practice of death, considering whether it will be here or be there, imagining the most sightly way of dying, and putting one's mind firmly in death. Although this may be a most difficult thing, if one will do it, it can be done. There is nothing that one should suppose cannot be done."[6]

That such a mindset should be axiomatic is demonstrated by Tsunetomo when he observes that a warrior should take the care to ensure he has a presentable appearance. "Even if you are aware that you may be struck down today and are firmly resolved to an inevitable death, if you are slain with an unseemly appearance, you will show your lack of previous resolve, will be despised by your enemy, and will appear unclean.

---

[3] *Hagakure*, 99.
[4] Ibid., 109.
[5] Ibid., 111.
[6] Ibid., 118.

For this reason, it is said that both old and young should take care of their appearance."[7]

Of one thing I am sure, a warrior's relation to death is intimate; we can be on all sides of it. Further, death cannot be avoided. When your number comes up, death comes to us all. How a warrior views death makes all the difference in how he lives and fights.

3. <u>The rule of seven breaths</u> (Hagakure, 62). According to Yamamoto Tsunetomo, one should make his decisions within the space of seven breaths. Lingering too long on a decision often leads to a state called paralysis by analysis, an inability to act due to an inability to make a decision. Such as state can complicate a small issue, and turn it into a big issue; if you are afraid of making a mistake, often not acting is an even bigger mistake. Tsunetomo observes:

Lord Takanobu said, "If discrimination is long, it will spoil." Lord Naoshige said, "When matters are done leisurely, seven out of ten will turn out badly. A warrior is a person who does things quickly." When your mind is going hither and thither, discrimination will never be brought to a conclusion. With an intense, fresh and unyielding spirit, one will make his judgments within the space of seven breaths. It is a matter of being determined and having the spirit to break right through to the other side.[8]

---

[7] Ibid., 31.
[8] Ibid., 62.

No doubt, the most excellent part of *Hagakure* is the short but poignant parable of the rainstorm. Tsunetomo writes:

There is something to be learned from a rainstorm. When meeting with a sudden shower, you try not to get wet and run quickly along the road. But doing such things as passing under the eaves of houses, you still get wet. When you are resolved from the beginning, you will not be perplexed, though you still get the same soaking. This understanding extends to everything.[9]

I believe if you get this, you understand the very essence of Bushido and gain an invaluable mindset prior to the fight. "Death is a risk of a soldier's trade."[10] If the way of the samurai is to live in the moment, firmly resolved to one's inevitable death, then the samurai become as one already dead. There is therefore nothing to fear. In such a mindset, coming back alive out of a battle, is nothing short of being reborn out of an inevitable death.

Mind you, this doesn't mean suicidal recklessness. The Samurai disdained that. Rather this is a mindset that fortifies the ideal warrior. Accepting death as a highly probable outcome, a samurai was able to fully give himself to the battle. If he was dead already, what was there to fear? Resolution to inevitable death gave a Samurai warrior freedom to give his all. This often was the defining factor leading to victory. Perhaps Bushido

---

9 Ibid., 40.
10 Neil Sheehan, *A Bright Shining Lie* (New York: Random House, 1988).

may be best summed up with the goal "to live and die well." That this quality of mental courage was lauded by the ancients is evidenced by every martial philosophy that has been handed down to us. Consider Shakespeare's words in *Julius Caesar*:

It seems to me most strange that men should fear;
Seeing that death, a necessary end,
Will come when it will come.

Likewise, in Shakespeare's *Hamlet*:

There is special providence in the fall of a sparrow.
If it be now, 'tis not to come;
if it be not to come, it will be now;
if it be not now, yet it will come. The readiness is all.

An ideal near akin to this thought, one which has fortified warriors down through the centuries is the Stoic understanding of Providence. The Roman philosopher Seneca once observed, "I know that everything is ordained and proceeds according to a law that endures forever. The fates guide us, and the length of every man's days is decided at the first hour of his birth: every cause depends upon some earlier cause: one long chain of destiny decides all things, public or private."[11] Such a mindset, Seneca goes on to say, puts steel in the soul of a warrior:

Do not, I beg you, shrink in fear from those things which the immortal gods apply like spurs, as it were, to our souls. Disaster is Virtue's opportunity. Justly may those be termed

---

[11] Seneca, *On Providence*.

unhappy who are dulled by an excess of good fortune, who rest, as it were, in dead calm upon a quiet sea; whatever happens we'll come to them as a change. Cruel fortune bears hardest upon the inexperienced; to the tender neck the yoke is heavy. The raw recruit turns pale at the thought of a wound, but the veteran looks undaunted upon his own gore, knowing that blood has often been the price of his victory.[12]

Likewise, Stonewall Jackson once remarked, "I will try and not go into danger unnecessarily. But each of us has his duty to perform, without regard to consequences; we must perform it and trust to Providence."[13]

For the Stoics, we should live are best lives fate permitting. Cicero explained this by way of the metaphor of the archer. An archer takes aim at a target and fires his arrow as skillfully as he can. Yet, once the arrow has left his bow, whether or not his arrow hits the target is in the hands of fate. As such, the Stoic ideal is to seek events to happen as they must, not so much as we will them to happen. In this way, we can accept victory or defeat with equanimity.

To be certain, this mindset is not always easily attained. General Patton echoed this sentiment. In a speech to his assembled troops, he said:

Men, all this stuff you hear about America not wanting to fight, wanting to stay out of the war, is a lot of horse dung. Americans love to fight. All real Americans love the sting and clash of

---

[12] Ibid.
[13] Henry K. Douglas, *I Rode with Stonewall* (Chapel Hill, NC: University of North Carolina Press, 1940), 102.

battle. When you were kids, you all admired the champion marble shooter, the fastest runner, the big-league ball players, and the toughest boxers. Americans love a winner and will not tolerate a loser. Americans play to win all the time. That's why Americans have never lost and will never lose a war. The very thought of losing is hateful to Americans. Battle is the most significant competition in which a man can indulge. It brings out all that is best, and it removes all that is base.

You are not all going to die. Only two percent of you right here today would be killed in a major battle. Every man is scared in his first action. If he says he's not, he's a g..damn liar. But the real hero is the man who fights even though he's scared. Some men will get over their fright in a minute under fire, some take an hour, and for some it takes days. But the real man never lets his fear of death overpower his honor, his sense of duty to his country, and his innate manhood.

Some of you men are wondering whether or not you'll chicken out under fire. Don't worry about it. I can assure you that you'll all do your duty. War is a bloody business, a killing business. The Nazis are the enemy. Wade into them, spill their blood or they will spill yours. Shoot them in the guts. Rip open their belly. When shells are hitting all around you and you wipe the dirt from your face and you realize that it's not dirt, it's the blood and guts of what was once your best friend, you'll know what to do.

In his book, *War As I Knew It*, Patton further added,

If we take the generally accepted definition of bravery as a quality which knows not fear, I have never seen a brave man. All men are frightened. The more intelligent they are, the more they are frightened. The courageous man is a man who forces himself, in spite of his fear, to carry on. Discipline, pride, self-respect, self-confidence, and the love of glory are attributes which will make a man courageous even when he is afraid.[14]

Then, in a motivational letter to his son, he wrote: "All men are timid on entering any fight. Whether it is the first or the last fight, all of us are timid. Cowards are those who let their timidity get the better of their manhood." In that vein, Churchill declared, "The brave man is not he who does not feel afraid, but he who conquers that fear."

There's another aspect to cowardice that warrants attention. Like courage, cowardice is a complex quality. It may be argued, the coward has an inability to experience what soldiers call comradery and *esprit de corps*. Lacking the ability to see himself as part of a body of men, and overly concerned with himself, and his safety, the coward has insufficient resources to overcome his dread of death. Philosopher Jesse Gray describes this in ways that few can. Before the monstrous reality of death:

The coward feels all the frailty and exposure of this existence, and senses that the struggle is an unequal one. Even temporary survival must be procured by careful stratagems and by yielding dignity here and there. Death is a personal enemy of his, a relentless, absolute, all-encompassing enemy. But the coward's inner poverty of life and love makes him no fit antagonist. I think it must be said that his fear is not to be separated from a dim recognition that he belongs to this opponent. In spite of himself, death is not remote from his inner self in all his impulses. The coward, unrelated to his fellows, has an insufficient hold on life and is not in charge of

---

[14] George S. Patton Jr., *War As I Knew It* (New York: Houghton Mifflin, 1947), 336.

himself or his fate. The brave man might fear death as an opponent possessing all the qualities opposite to those which he himself possesses. His discipline in the face of this enemy is governed by the recognition that death is implacable and will ultimately triumph in an outward sense. But for the coward, death is within him. He is related to this most gruesome enemy, and the more he struggles to escape, the greater is his captivity. When the coward's body is finally yielded up to death, there is nothing instructive or solemn about the spectacle. Few scenes are more deeply unpleasant.[15]

It was for this reason that Napoleon once remarked that courage drives FEAR into the enemy's ranks.

Just how a man conquers his fears is often debated. As the many volumes on war attest, fear is ever present on a battlefield, it's the uncontrolled fear that is detestable and destructive.

In my opinion, mental courage is a mental resolve to go despite danger. As psychologists suggest, fear is an emotional reaction to real danger, while anxiety is an imagined fear. Perhaps the best answer as to how best to conquer fear can be seen in the difference between fear and anxiety. In the Greek, these words are *phobos* (fear) and *merimnao* (anxiety). Phobos means "to flee," literally, "withdraw." Simple enough. On the other hand, the word for anxiety, gives us a nuance. In the Greek, *merimnao* literally means "split mind." It seems the best way to conquer fear and go on is to avoid a split mind. In other words, avoid imagined fears, and have the

---

[15] J. Glenn Gray, *The Warriors: Reflections on Men in Battle* (New York: Bison, 1970), 115.

discipline to stay in the present, and be firmly resolved in your inevitable death. After all, we're the ones who run to the sound of the guns!

Earlier, I mentioned the Stoic philosopher Zeno. He had this to say regarding death. "No evil is glorious. But there are cases of glorious death. Death therefore is not evil." On the battlefield, the real enemy is fear. Fear can keep a man out of danger, but courage supports him in it. Courage is simply fear that has said its prayers.

Alvin York

One of the bravest men to ever serve in the Armed Forces of the United States was once thought a coward. Drafted into the US Army in 1917 to serve in the war against Germany, Alvin C. York was a man who was having difficulties reconciling his Christian beliefs with what he was being called up to do. A native of Pall Mall, Tennessee, York was raised in a Christian home. The Army life was an effective check to his licentiousness. In February 1918, he completed basic training and was assigned to the 82nd Infantry Division (later to be the 82nd Airborne Division).

As his unit was approaching time for its deployment, York's religious qualms got the better of him. Believing killing in combat to be a sin led him to claim "conscientious objector" status. He had before requested to be dismissed from the service on such religious grounds, but his request was denied. As the issue reached a definitive point, York was summoned to stand before his battalion commander, Major Buxton. Himself also a devout Christian, Buxton, weighed in with Scriptural support for the just war theory. York was given a ten-day leave to think things over. It was during this sabbatical in Pall Mall that York felt at peace regarding what he must do. "If a man can make peace by fighting," York said, "he is a peacemaker."

By the summer of 1918, York's unit, the 328th Infantry Regiment, found itself in the trenches facing the Germans. On October 8, 1918, York's Regiment took part in the Allied attack to capture the German-held Hill 223, near Chatel-Chéhéry, France. As York recounts:

The Germans got us, and they got us right smart. They just stopped us dead in our tracks. Their machine guns were up there on the heights overlooking us and well hidden, and we couldn't tell for certain where the terrible heavy fire was coming from. And I'm telling you they were shooting straight. Our boys just went down like the long grass before the mowing machine at home. Our attack just faded out. And there we were, lying down, about halfway across the valley and those German machine guns and big shells were getting us hard.

As the forward platoons of the 328th advanced, they got pinned down by the German machine guns. York, and thirteen others, were launched out from the main body to silence the guns on the hill. The patrol managed to infiltrate the German lines unscathed. Behind enemy lines, the patrol worked its way through the woods, and stumbled upon a German headquarters. A large group of German soldiers were caught eating their breakfast. After a few warning shots the Germans surrendered, and the American patrol formed their POWs into a line.

Suddenly, German machine gun fire from the upper ridge erupted killing six men and wounding three others, including the patrol leader. This placed York in command of seven able bodied men. Sizing up the situation, York recounts:

Those machine guns were spitting fire and cutting down the undergrowth all around me something awful. And the Germans were yelling orders. You never heard such a racket in all of your life. I didn't have time to dodge behind a tree or dive into the brush. As soon as the machine guns opened fire on me, I began to exchange shots with them. There were over thirty of them in continuous action, and all I could do was touch the Germans off just as fast as I could.

The whole event reminded York of turkey shoots back home. However, as York later recounted:

The German's heads were a lot bigger than turkeys. In order to sight me in," says York, "the Germans had to show their heads. Whenever a head popped up, I just touched it off. I didn't want to kill any more than I had to. But it was they or I.

There are types of warriors who consider death a reality for others but not themselves. Believing, in a sense, that they are impervious to spraying bullets and exploding shells. For such, the ground on which they stand is believed to be secure by their standing on it. Death robs others, but not them. Jesse Glenn Gray describes the courage of such warriors:

Free from anxiety, they are frequently able to see the ridiculous and amusing aspects of combat life that provide much priceless cheer and humor for their comrades. Fortunate is the unit that can count one or more of these soldiers in its ranks; and in fact, most units do appear to contain them. They are a perennial phenomenon in war, a cause of wonder and admiration, as though their like had never been. Sometimes they become the subject of war tales, which quickly takes on mythlike proportions. If such soldiers command men, as frequently happens, they have the capacity to inspire the troops to deeds of recklessness and self-sacrifice.[16]

York was such a type. When he ran out of rifle ammunition, he transitioned to his Colt .45 pistol. When a German lieutenant led a bayonet charge against him, York saw the six men coming and quickly applied another Pall Mall shooting lesson, hunting ducks. York learned that if he shot the lead bird in a formation first, the others would scatter. But if he shot the birds back to front, the others would keep flying and give him clean targets. Even though the bayonet charge was already dangerously close, York fired at the last man in the line first and dropped them all in rapid succession. The lead man he dropped last as he was nearly within a bayonet length.

Watching in astonishment as York was annihilating his unit, the German commander surrendered. York and his seven men promptly marched one hundred and thirty-two German prisoners back to the American lines. In the fierce firefight, twenty-five Germans died, and thirty-five machine guns were put out of action. French Marshal Foch told York, "What you did was the greatest thing accomplished by any private soldier of all the armies of

---

[16] J. Glenn Gray, *The Warriors: Reflections on Men in Battle* (New York: Bison, 1970), 106.

Europe." Who can match an inspired marksman who believes that God is with him? For his courageous action, Sergeant Alvin C. York was later awarded the Congressional Medal of Honor.

Courage in warriors takes various forms, as does views of death. For the adventurous type, death is the last journey to be experienced, for the professional soldier, it's the last mission to be accomplished, and for the philosophical soldier, it's the last bit of knowledge to be attained. Regardless of one's viewpoint, death is the last enemy. Only the dead see the end of war.

Mutual Courage

There's another form of courage that has a collective quality. Underscoring its utmost importance, and having seen fighting units destroyed, Clausewitz once observed, "once a fighting unit has lost its collective courage, it can be "dragged down to the brutish world where danger is shirked, and shame is unknown." It was for this reason that Napoleon once remarked that in war, the moral is to the physical three to one. As such courage is not only the collective spirit that animates a fighting force, but it can also save an element from catastrophe.

Understanding this, and emphasizing the utmost importance of mutual courage, WWII General Samuel L. A. (SLAM) Marshall observed,

It is of the battlefield, as I have defined it earlier, that I speak in saying that the mind of the infantry soldier should be conditioned to an understanding of its reality through all stages of his training. He needs to be taught the nature of that field as it is in war and as he may experience it someday. For if he does not acquire soldiers view of the field, his image of it will be formed from the reading of novels or the romance written by war correspondence, more from viewing the battlefield as it is imagined to be by Hollywood. One of the purposes of training should be to remove these false ideas of battle from his mind... it is possible that the infantry soldier can be trained to anticipate fully the true conditions of the battlefield; It is possible that units can be schooled to take full and prompt action against the disunity dying effect of these conditions. Fears ever present, but it is uncontrolled fear that is the enemy of successful operation, and the control of fear depends upon the extent to which all dangers of distractions may be correctly anticipated and therefore understood. The heart of the matter is to relate the man to his fellow soldier as he will find him on the field of combat, to condition him to human nature as he will learn to depend on it when the ground offers him no comfort and weapons fail.

Only when the human rather than the material, aspects of operation are put uppermost can tactical bodies be conditioned to make the most of the potential unity. It is beyond question that the most serious and repeated breakdowns on the field of combat are caused by failure of the controls over human nature. In minor tactics the utmost variable cause of local defeat is fundamentally the shrinkage of fire. On the field of fire it is the touch of human nature which gives men courage and enables them to make proper use of their weapons depriving of this vitalizing spark an omen would go forward against enemy. I hold it to be one of the most simplest truths of war that the thing which enables an infantry soldier to keep going with his weapons is the near presence or the presumed presence of a comrade.

The warmth which derived from human companionship is as essential to his employment of the arms with which he fights as is the finger with which he pulls a trigger or the eye with which he aligns his sights. The other man may be almost beyond hailing or seeing distance, but he must be there somewhere within a man's consciousness with the onset of demoralization is almost immediate and very quickly the mind begins to despair turns to thoughts of escape. In this condition he is no longer a fighting individual, and though he holds to his weapon, it is little better than a club. It is that way with any fighting man. He is sustained by his fellows primarily and by his weapons secondarily. Having to make a choice in the face of the enemy, he would rather be unarmed with his comrades around him then altogether alone, though possessing the most perfect of quick firing weapons.[17]

Prisoners of war from the Vietnam War, some of which endured as much as seven or more years of captivity, say that the most effective tool their captors used against them was isolation. Prisoners who could communicate with each other generally fared better, despite physical torture, than those who were completely cut off from their fellow captives. This collective experience underscores the importance that mutual courage can have.

Admiral James B. Stockdale was a Navy fighter pilot in the Vietnam War. On September 9, 1965, as commanding officer of Carrier Air Group Commander (CAG-16), Stockdale was catapulted from the deck of the USS Oriskany for what would be his final mission. Shot down over the skies of Hanoi, he wound up in the infamous

---

[17] Samuel L. A. Marshall, *Men Against Fire: The Problem of Battle Command* (Oklahoma City: University of Oklahoma press, 1947), 39-40.

"Hanoi Hilton" where he spent the next seven and a half years under unimaginably brutal conditions. As he parachuted into enemy hands, he said to himself, "I'm leaving behind the world of technology and entering the world of Epictetus." Stockdale took the core thoughts of Stoicism into the hellhole of Hanoi Hilton. The words of Epictetus put steel in his heart and mind. He observes,

So, I took those core thoughts into prison. I also remembered a lot of attitude-shaping remarks from the *Enchiridion* on how not to kid yourself into thinking that you can somehow stand aloof, be an "observer of the passing scene," aloof from the prisoner underground organization. Enchiridion 17: Remember that you are an actor in a drama of such sort as the Author chooses: if short, then in a short one; if long, then in a long one. If it be His pleasure that you should enact a poor man, or a cripple, or a ruler, or a private citizen, see that you act it well. For this is your business, to act well the given part. But to choose it belongs to Another.[18]

Despite being physically tortured, kept in solitary confinement for four years, including having his legs in irons for two years, Stockdale organized a system of communication and developed a cohesive set of rules that not only governed prisoner behavior but also kept the men's spirits alive. Drawing largely from principles of Stoic philosophy, Stockdale's system was codified in the acronym BACK US, meaning don't Bow, stay off the Air, admit no Crimes, never Kiss them goodbye and Unity over Self. These rules gave prisoners a sense of hope and

---

[18] Stockdale on Stoicism I: *The Stoic Warrior's Triad.*

empowerment. In fact, many credited these rules as giving them the strength to endure their lengthy ordeal.

As a parting shot to an assembled Marine Aviator audience at Camp Quantico, Stockdale finished his remarks with the following:

I think more needs to be said about good and evil. After all, the Stoic is indifferent to everything but good and evil. In Stoic thought, our good and our evil come from the same locus. "Vice and virtue reside in the will alone." Learning to take charge of your emotions is empowering. When you get there, Enchiridion 30 applies: "No one can harm you without your permission." And by "harm" Epictetus means, as Stoics always mean, harming your inner self, your self-respect, and your obligation to be faithful. He can break your arm or your leg, but not to worry. They'll heal. This is called the coherence of Stoicism, and Cicero used this as the basis of his founding of Natural Law and International Law. "True law is right reason in agreement with nature." The Stoics were good citizens. In politics the Stoic would love his country and hold himself ready to die at any time to avert its disgrace or his own. But a man's conscience was to be higher than any law. A man has a right to be responsible, self-ruling, autonomous.

So, on good and evil, where does that leave us? Nothing that is natural can be evil. Death cannot be evil. Disease cannot be evil. Natural disasters cannot be evil. Nothing inevitable can be evil. The universe as a whole is perfect, and everything in it has a place in the overall design. Inevitability is produced by the workings of this mechanism. Events do not happen by chance, they arrive by appointment. There is a cause for everything, and "chance" is simply a name for undiscovered causes. Remember: Controlling your emotions can be empowering. Your inner self is what you make it. Refuse to want to fear, and you start acquiring a constancy of character that makes it impossible for another to do you wrong.[19]

Moral Courage

In chapter two I discussed the My Lai massacre and how it was a dark page in US history. What is not as well-known is the pilot who curtailed the massacre. Flying in support of the "operations" going on in My Lai, helicopter pilot Warrant Officer Hugh Thompson scanned the ground below. As he recounts,

We kept flying back and forth, reconning in front and in the rear, and it didn't take very long until we started noticing the large number of bodies everywhere. Everywhere we'd look, we'd see bodies. These were infants, two, three, four, five-year-olds, women, very old men, no draft-age people whatsoever. Then we saw a young girl about twenty years old lying on the grass. We could see that she was unarmed and wounded in the chest. We marked her with smoke because we saw a squad not too far away. The smoke was green, meaning it's safe to approach. Red would have meant the opposite. We were hovering six feet off the ground not more than twenty feet away when Captain Medina came over, kicked her, stepped back, and finished her off. He did it right in front of us. When we saw Medina do that, it clicked. It was our guys doing the killing.

Right after the execution, Thompson discovered an irrigation ditch full of Lieutenant Calley's victims. Thompson then radioed a message to accompanying gunships and Task Force Barker headquarters, "It looks to me like there's an awful lot of unnecessary killing going

---

[19] Ibid.

on down there. Something ain't right about this. There are bodies everywhere. There's a ditch full of bodies that we saw. There's something wrong here."[20] When Thompson spotted civilians in the irrigation ditch, he immediately landed to assist the victims. He and Calley exchanged some heated words. He told Calley to help him get the villagers out. Calley replied the only help they would get was a hand grenade.

Obeying his convictions, Thompson placed his chopper down in front of the advancing American soldiers and gave his gunner, Lawrence Colburn, a simple, direct order: "Train your M-60 on the GIs. If they try to harm the villagers, open up on them." Thompson then radioed two gunships, and together they air-lifted a dozen villagers to safety, including a two-year old that Colburn cradled.

The My Lai massacre left some 500 Vietnamese civilians dead. As related by Trent Angers, "Concerned, senior American Division officers cancelled similar planned operations by Task Force Barker against other villages." This no doubt prevented the additional massacre of further hundreds, if not thousands, of Vietnamese civilians.[21]

It is noteworthy that some members of Calley's platoon realized the "enemy" they were attacking in the village

---

[20] Trent Angers, *The Forgotten Hero of My Lai: The Hugh Thompson Story* (New York: Acadian House, 2014), 77.
[21] Ibid., 219. Recently released evidence describes an additional 320 such incidents that were perpetrated in South Vietnam and Cambodia against civilians.

were in reality civilians. As was the case, they refused to shoot. As related by machine gunner Private Maples, Calley ordered him to use his machine gun on the Vietnamese in the ditch, but he refused. Another soldier, Dennis Conti, testified that he was ordered to round up people, mostly women and children, and bring them back to Calley on the trail south of the hamlet. As recounted by Conti, "Calley told us to make them squat down and bunch up so they couldn't get up and run. Minutes later Calley and another soldier, Paul Meadlo, who failed to question the unlawful order, fired directly into the people. There were burst and shots for two minutes. The people screamed and yelled and fell." Calley was later convicted of twenty-two counts of premeditated murder and was sentenced to be confined at hard labor for the length of his natural life. As a psychological casualty of the My Lai massacre, Thompson suffered from post-traumatic stress disorder which devastated him.

Christopher Kolenda rightly observes, "Just as we develop physical courage by experiencing and functioning under physical fear and moral courage by making the choice of right amidst the pressure to do otherwise, so we develop intellectual courage through the discomfort and ambiguity of experiencing ideas that challenge our depth and perspective."[22]

---

[22] Kolenda, *Leadership: The Warrior's Art*, xvii.

Principles of Courage

"Courage is half the victory."[1] It's the virtue that puts steel in our spines and helps us see through the fog of war and navigate the way to victory. Here are two principles:

Know: <u>Courage is every virtue at its testing point.</u>

Do: <u>Sense danger but embrace it willingly.</u> The greatest fear of the ideal warrior is not losing his life, but rather to bring dishonor to one's unit and the Nation.

There's simply no escape when God decides your days are numbered. In light of this law that endures forever, I submit to you that "dying before going into battle," recognizes that true honor lies in fulfilling Heaven's decree and no death incurred in so doing is shameful or

---

[1] *The Saga of Harald Hardrade*, Chapter 103.

disgraceful, rather it is honorable. And courage is action despite the fear of death. It's the virtue of courage that enables warriors to sacrifice all their tomorrows for our Nation's todays.

Introspection

I have purposely bookended each chapter with five introspective questions. These are designed to promote professional growth:

1. Do you have what it takes to stand when others can't or won't?

2. Do you have the guts to speak up for what's right?

3. What do you love about life?

4. Have you considered what your own death would be like?

5. What do you think is the worst thing that could happen to you?

The Battle of Cowpens, January 17, 1781.

7

Mental Fitness

"The soldier above all others prays for peace, for it is the soldier who must suffer and bear the deepest wounds and scars of war." – General Douglas MacArthur

Combat is one of the most intense situations the body, mind, and soul can experience. The complex nature of events in war is far beyond the normal range of human experience. As combat is joined, primordial impulses predominate, bringing out the very best and worst in all of us. There's a memorable quote from the movie *Edge of Tomorrow*. Bill Paxton's character, Master Sergeant Farell says, "Battle is the great redeemer. The fiery crucible in which the only true heroes are forged. The one place where all men truly share the same rank regardless of what kind of parasitic scum they were going in." This is most certainly truth. Somewhere, perhaps very near, a group of armed men will gladly kill you if they have the chance. No doubt a man can comfortably advise others from a safe position. But as you get closer to the enemy, you will of necessity, experience a sensation of danger that will be impossible to ignore. Added to this is the anticipation of killing another man and the utmost need of cheating death.

For the warrior class, violence is not only a possibility, but also a distinct feature of the calling. In light of this, like physical fitness, and tactical prowess, the conditions for success to be made before the fight must also include a mental preparedness. Sun Tzu put it this way, every battle is won or lost before it is fought. The key is entering combat with mental fitness. I want to outline this concept under three headings, the crucible of war, the casualties of war, and the conservation in war.

The Crucible of War

A crucible is a severe test or trial. It's an extremely challenging experience. War is the absolute crucible. It brings out the very best and worst in everyone. Patton rightly described war as an orgy of chaos. In such an environment, as we face threats, a complex series of things happen within us. Understanding this helps get our minds prepared for action.

When we encounter a threat, our brain commands a response from the body that is instantly executed. Our sympathetic nervous system (SNS) reacts by releasing hormones into our body and extra blood to our muscles that we will need to survive. First, our brain processes the information through sensory organs in the amygdala and hippocampus. The amygdala sees the significance of what's going on and alerts the brain. The hippocampus, which stores emotional memory, then categorizes and filters the threat through an emotional lens to evaluate it.

Receiving input from the hippocampus, the cingulate cortex makes a decision, activating the hypothalamus-pituitary-adrenal (HPA) - axis. This results in the release of "powerful stress hormones, including cortisol and adrenaline, which increase heart rate, blood pressure, and rate of breathing, preparing us to fight back or run away."[1] Adrenaline payout then gives us a huge surge in energy. Our body follows up with cortisol for continued alertness. This whole process takes a matter of seconds.

Added to these natural reactions to the threat of life, are the accumulated effects of killing others, death of comrades and leaders, inadequate sleep, the threat of improvised explosive devices (IEDs) and friendly-fire, so-called green on blue incidents, hard living conditions, handling dead bodies and body parts, and a myriad of other unpleasant experiences, such as smelling a burning dead body. In a battle, which can last for days on end, our sympathetic nervous system can be severely taxed, leading us to develop symptoms of battle fatigue and combat stress.

---

[1] Bessel A. Van der Kolk, *The Body Keeps the Score: Brain, Mind, And Body in The Healing of Trauma* (New York: Penguin Books, 2015), 61.

War is a crucible in which the body is naturally taxed. As such, it can leave us with some of the following effects:

1. Having difficulty falling asleep or staying asleep.
2. Having recurrent, vivid nightmares.
3. Feeling intense guilt or shame.
4. Feeling emotionally despondent.
5. Experiencing attacks of panic or rage.
6. Losing the ability to think rationally and clearly.
7. Feeling unable to enjoy pleasurable activities.
8. Losing confidence in previously held moral values.[2]

The above are normal effects. If and as these symptoms arise, we can and should reset ourselves mentally and emotionally before we allow ourselves to become imbalanced.

German novelist Erich Remarque is famous for his visceral descriptions of the First World War. In his book, *All Quiet on the Western Front*, Remarque describes what can happen if these effects mount without reset. He states:

The tension has worn us out. It is a deadly tension that feels as if a jagged knife blade is being scraped along the spine. Our legs won't function, our hands are trembling and our bodies are like thin membranes stretched over barely repressed madness, holding in what would otherwise be an unrestrained outburst of endless screams.

Comrade, I did not want to kill you. But you were only an idea to me before, an abstraction that lived in my mind and called

---

[2] Adopted from *Managing Combat and Operational Stress*.

forth its appropriate response. I thought of your hand-grenades, of your bayonet, of your rifle; now I see your wife and your face and our fellowship. Forgive me, comrade. We always see it too late. Why do they never tell us that you are poor devils like us, that your mothers are just as anxious as ours, and that we have the same fear of death, and the same dying and the same agony—Forgive me, comrade; how could you be my enemy?

I am young, I am twenty years old; yet I know nothing of life but despair, death, fear, and fatuous superficiality cast over an abyss of sorrow. I see how peoples are set against one another, and in silence, unknowingly, foolishly, obediently, innocently slay one another.

He fell in October 1918, on a day that was so quiet and still on the whole front, that the army report confined itself to the single sentence: All quiet on the Western Front. He had fallen forward and lay on the earth as though sleeping. Turning him over one saw that he could not have suffered long; his face had an expression of calm, as though almost glad the end had come.

How senseless is everything that can ever be written, done, or thought, when such things are possible. It must be all lies and of no account when the culture of a thousand years could not prevent this stream of blood being poured out, these torture-chambers in their hundreds of thousands. A hospital alone shows what war is.

As a soldier who has seen some of the ravages of war, I must say that Erich Remarque certainly had a way with words, particularly an ability to describe with words sights, sounds, and smells of things that "hold the horror of the world."

Additionally, the atmosphere of war is filled with such highs and lows, that a man fully absorbed in it experiences the sensations of riding a most exhilarating, emotional rollercoaster. War also compresses the greatest opposites into the shortest time. "The alternation of dullness and excitement," writes Jesse Glenn Gray, "in their in extreme degrees separates war from peace."[3] The veteran soldier describes the highs and lows of the moment his unit liberated a French town from the Nazis:

In the delirium of liberation, many individuals were constantly going from a group that was hugging and kissing returned FFI (French Forces of the Interior) comrades to join another that were torturing isolated collaborators. We could observe love and hatred, tenderness and brutality, succeed each other and many a person within moments. Excitement was at a fever pitch. German soldiers with hands high in the air were being marched to a prisoner collection point by triumphant boys. With a sense of horror, a comrade and I walking the streets watched a group beating a girl whose hair had been crudely sheared off in her face bloodied and bruised. She was crying bitterly as her tormentors kicked her along, taunting and jeering and hooting; Evidently, she had been the mistress of some German and possibly had spied on the local resistance. A little further on we saw a man, with his face cut, running like a hurt and frightened beast before men who were doing worse things to him than were happening to the girl. It was clear that he had no chance of remaining alive if and when his pursuers cornered him.

---

[3] J. Glenn Gray, *The Warriors: Reflections on Men in Battle* (New York: Bison, 1970), 12.

Suddenly from a group perhaps 20 yards ahead of us a girl detached herself and ran directly toward me. Slim and fleet as a deer, she was in my startled arms before I knew what was happening. A hug, a quick kiss on the mouth, and she spun away with flaming cheeks into another crowd and scarcely the time it takes to draw breath. Everybody laughed happily and applauded, while I picked up my fallen cap and tried to conceal my red face and inner confusion. The act was purely spontaneous; Doubtless, in her excitement she hardly knew what she was doing. Nothing could be more typical of the confused emotions of war than that town and the first few hours of freedom from German occupation. There were other kinds of excitement, not so gleeful, in which the nervous tension was, if possible, even greater. Perhaps no soldier could describe adequately his feelings on a D-Day landing on the fire. Moods of fear, anticipation, helplessness, praying and cursing, adventure and longing succeed each other like lightning. Inhuman cruelty can give way to superhuman kindness. Inhibitions vanish, and people are reduced to their essence. If afterward they seem quickly to forget, perhaps the memory is not wholly lost. Again and again in moments of this kind I was as such inspired by the nobility of some of my fellows as appalled by the animality of others, or, more exactly, by both qualities and the same person. The average degree, which we commonly know in peacetime, conceals as much as it reveals about the human creature.[4]

Along with these authors, what I have discovered is the alien character of war experiences can leave an indelible mark on the soul. I too have experienced what may be referred to as "being on all sides of death," looking death in the face on more occasions than one. It goes without

---

[4] *The Warriors*, 14-15.

saying then that exposure to war can cause serious psychological consequences. For many veterans, it's a story of war finding them, yet never leaving them the same. It is my belief that prevention is the best cure. Be it as it may, having a mental preparedness that understands these complexities and effects will help us put our best foot forward.

So far, in our discussion on war and the virtues that make excellent warriors we have covered a lot of ground. One thing that remains is moving on after a traumatic event. After the "hurly-burly is done, when the battle is lost and won," you will have to move on with your life. Just how that is done isn't always easy. You may experience some lingering effects of what you had to live through. Afterall, you may have to kit up and go out again.

The Casualties of War

What I want to do here is discuss the very worst that can happen and how to prevent it. There's a host of mighty warriors in Homer's *Iliad*. Perhaps the most tragic of all in that epic is a warrior named Ajax. As I've argued, honor is a prize to be one and guarded as it can easily be lost. As it is said, a good name is hard won and easily tarnished. Losing honor can have devastating effects. In Sophocles' tragedy *Ajax*, the hero suffers what I call a catastrophic loss of honor. Odysseus and Ajax argue over who should receive the armor of the dead hero Achilles.

Fashioned by Hephaestus himself, the armor would indeed honor its recipient as the greatest warrior after

Achilles. The Greeks make the Trojan captives vote as to who is to receive the armor. It is awarded to Odysseus. Enraged, Ajax vows to kill the Greek leaders Menelaus and Agamemnon. But Ajax is tricked into believing that the sheep that have been taken as spoils of war are actually the Greek leaders. Unwittingly, he slaughters the animals which he believes are his rivals.

When he finally comes to his senses, Ajax is shocked and ashamed over his actions. In great shame, he laments, "Look at me! Me, the brave hero! The one who never trembles with fear in battle! Never afraid of enemies! Look at what I've done! Look at me! Is there anyone more shameful than me? Is there anyone who's suffered a greater insult?"

His wife, Tecmessa, pleads with him not to leave her and her child. Ajax pretends to be moved. Then says he is going out to purify himself and to bury the sword given to him by Hector. By the time he is found, Ajax has buried the sword in his own guts. Tragically, an alarming number of veterans follow in his footsteps. War is a crucible. It causes trauma that can undo a warrior's character. Sophocles' *Ajax* is a great example of a traumatized warrior.

In 2002, an ugly incident occurred which has sadly become all too familiar. In a period of about six weeks, four Special Operations soldiers who had returned from Afghanistan murdered their wives. Two of the soldiers killed themselves as well. One man had moved out of the house and was living in the barracks. While the specific motives remain unresolved, on the surface it appears that combat trauma got the better of these men. Another possibility lies in the anti-malarial drug mefloquine, also called Lariam. All four of the men were taking it. Used by the Army in deployments, this drug has been known to cause a person to become psychotic. Many are convinced that this drug was a factor in the brutal murders.

This year I was horrified to learn that three of my former teammates had killed themselves. I was shocked. They had served with distinction, had families, and what appeared to be successful careers. Together, we had accomplished an amazing feat. We graduated from the Operator Training Course, walked across the hall, as they say, to serve in the Unit. I'm not sure what caused them to take their own lives. Tragically, an alarming number of veterans, to the rate of twenty-one per day, follow in their footsteps.

Now, I am not certain why my former teammates took their own lives, and, in one instance, the life of his wife as well, but as we know, veterans often suffer from what is referred to as posttraumatic stress (PTS), and posttraumatic stress disorder (PTSD). Brought on by a variety of distressing events, including combat, as well as physical or sexual violence, trauma is a type of damage to the mind. In the Greek, trauma literally means wound. Psychological trauma is therefore a wounding of the soul.

Posttraumatic stress (PTS) involves having intense, disturbing thoughts and feelings related to experiences that last long after the traumatic event has ended. The type of symptoms that will present varies from person to person and most likely is based on their personal history and the nature of the trauma they have experienced. Related to PTS, is posttraumatic stress disorder (PTSD). PTSD is "a disorder in which a person experiences trauma-related symptoms or impairments in everyday functioning that lasts for at least a month and sometimes for life."[5]

PTSD

PTSD may occur in those who have "experienced, witnessed, or otherwise been confronted with an event or events that involved actual or threatened death, serious injury, or sexual violence."[6] Such traumatic events may encompass a wide array of experiences. These events may include rape or child sexual abuse, natural disasters, serious accidents, combat, including those who have been threatened with sexual violence, serious injury or death. A 2004 study from Walter Reed Army Institute of Research found that 17% of those returning from Iraq suffered from symptoms related to PTSD within three months of their return.[7]

The trauma is stored, and the body keeps the score. PTSD also encompasses second order affects, bringing about severe impairment in social or occupational

---

[5] Matthew J. Friedman, *Posttraumatic and Acute Stress Disorders, Sixth Edition* (New York: Springer, 2015), 15.
[6] D. H. Barlow, *Clinical handbook of Psychological Disorders: A Step-by-Step Treatment Manual* (New York: Guilford, 2014), 62.
[7] Nancy Sherman, *Stoic Warriors: The Ancient Philosophy Behind the Military Mind* (New York: Oxford, 2005), ix.

functioning. Moreover, due to the rippling effect of trauma, family, friends, and whole communities can be affected. A textbook case would be that of a Vietnam veteran reliving the moment his platoon was ambushed as a car backfires. The resulting intrusively recollective sound triggers a particular flashback which in turn causes him to momentarily lose touch with reality and crash his car.

The type of symptoms vary. People may experience PTSD symptoms within one month of a traumatic event. However, in a delayed onset, symptoms may not appear until years later. The trauma is stored, and the body keeps the score. These symptoms can cause significant problems with normal everyday life, impacting social relationships and one's ability to hold down a job.

Symptoms of PTSD are divided into four basic clusters consisting of re-experiencing, avoiding/numbing, hyperarousal, and negative cognitions. Just which symptoms will present appears to vary by type of traumatic experience, with no simple straight correlation.

Re-experiencing is when the individual relives the traumatic event. This can be in the form of a nightmare, flashback and can cause physiological stress and reactivity. While reliving their traumatic experience, "individuals may feel that they are in danger in the immediate moment. They may panic and want to escape. They may become aggressive or assaultive in order to protect themselves from the reexperience of threat."[8] Flashbacks and dreams are the two most prominent forms of the re-experiencing symptom. "The content of nightmares typically involves the traumatic experience and occurs during REM sleep but has been observed during sleep onset."[9]

Those with avoidance symptoms may become numb, and at times completely avoid anything associated with the traumatic events. Hyperarousal causes a person to remain always on alert. Such hypervigilance may be seen as an attempt to avoid becoming a victim again. Such a state can drain a person biologically and psychologically so that "emotions are heightened and aroused, and even minor events may produce a state in which the heart pounds rapidly, muscles are tense, and there is great overall agitation."[10] As noted by psychologists, those with hyperarousal symptoms lose more sleep than those suffering with other symptom clusters.

Those in the wake of trauma may experience negative thoughts or feelings. This may include irritable and angry feelings, a persistent negative mood, fear, sadness, as well as guilt, anxiety or shame. All of these symptoms can cause sleep difficulties, exaggerated responses, irritability, outbursts of anger, and poor concentration.

After a traumatic event many find it difficult to stop thinking about what happened. They may develop

---

[8] A. Cash, *Wiley Concise Guides to Mental Health: Posttraumatic Stress Disorder* (New York: John Wiley & Sons, 2005), 40.
[9] Ibid.
[10] *Posttraumatic and Acute Stress Disorders*, 18.

various trauma reactions to cope with the stress. One that I have seen repeatedly in the military is referred to as trauma pleasure. This reaction is defined as seeking or finding pleasure and stimulation in the presence of extreme danger, violence, or risk. Such things are done to gain control over what is perceived to be out of control. This type of reaction involves engaging in thrill seeking behaviors which may include high-risk activities like skydiving, driving a car or riding a motorcycle at extremely fast and dangerous speeds. Other modes of this reaction include the use of illegal drugs, associating with dangerous people, gambling, and seeking dangerous self-destructive behavior, including unsafe sexual encounters.

According to the Center for Substance Abuse Treatment (2014), this reaction is a conscious or subconscious reenactment of an aspect of the trauma. In other words, reacting in this way, PTSD sufferers place themselves into various adrenaline-filled dangerous situations in an effort to gain control or mastery over that aspect of the traumatic event. As a veteran of the wars in Iraq and Afghanistan, I have scores of friends who have bought Harleys and have ridden them like they stole it. The danger to physical reenactment is obvious. Moreover, cognitively reliving such traumatic scenarios can come to dominate a person's life and be as equally dangerous.

A famous example of this reaction to trauma comes by way of the film, *The Deer Hunter*. In the film, the character Nick, played by Christopher Walken, and Michael, played by Robert De Niro are best friends. As the war in Vietnam is raging, they both join the Army. In one scene, they are both captured by the Vietcong and are made to play Russian roulette. They sit across from each other as each in turn are forced to play the dangerous game. They survive the ordeal when Michael asks for three bullets instead of one. Michael bets with his life that the chamber of the pistol he holds to his head is empty. He grimaces as he pulls the trigger. Surviving near death, Michael blasts his way out of captivity, firing the three bullets at the nearby guards, saving Nick and another friend. Together they are rescued. However, the body keeps the score.

Michael recovers and returns to America, but Nick cannot let go of the event and remains in Vietnam. When Michael goes back to Vietnam to get Nick, he finds him playing Russian roulette for money. Arguably, Nick is reenacting the event in an effort to free himself from the traumatic event, or at least gain mastery over it. At the climax of the film, Michael once again faces Nick across a table at Russian roulette. Michael desperately tries to bring Nick back from his captivity. He wants to save him from this most dangerous game. But he can't. Sadly, Nick's inability to let go has a deadly price.

The simple point that is often overlooked is posttraumatic stress is moral injury. Many react to traumatic events like Nick. It is a known fact that those with PTSD are five times more likely to die from suicide. I had a friend who deployed nine times to Iraq and Afghanistan. He never shared the fact he was struggling, and eventually killed himself. He was able to present a remarkable façade, all the while he was suffering terribly within. When I learned of his death, I was furious. I would have driven thousands of miles to help him if he had only called.

In addition to those who have taken their own lives, I know scores of men who self-medicate. Wanting to avoid the recurrent painful thoughts and feelings, perhaps suffering from what is called "survivor guilt," many take to alcohol or drugs to self-sooth. Doing so is not only self-destructive, but it also prevents you from fully addressing the traumatic experience and blunts recovery. Recognizing PTSD, and other related trauma-related symptoms is critical.

As a known fact, PTSD is notoriously stigmatized in the Army. In Army rationale, PTSD is a death sentence for a career. In the military, there is a sad truth that virtually no one talks about. First, normally, everyone in charge is working towards a zero-defect unit standing. Those in charge are looking to make the next grade. In their thinking, problems reflect poor leadership. Second, when it comes to PTS and PTSD, everyone knows this and does not want to be the one who looks weak.

The result is, a sort of "don't ask, don't tell" mentality prevails. Most units return from a deployment, put their people on a short leave, and then get ready for the next deployment (The pattern my buddy who took his own life fell into). As such, it's imperative for everyone in a unit to check up on others for signs of combat stress, PTS, and

PTSD. We have to love people enough to be there and intervene when necessary.

Between October 2001 and August 2021, approximately 1.75 million US troops deployed in Iraq and Afghanistan. In many cases, exposure to combat amongst many of those deployed took a psychological toll. In fact, as noted by psychologists, the combat-related stress over multiple rotations are disproportionately high compared with the physical injuries of combat. In light of this, some exposed to the ravages of war will undoubtedly experience some form of trauma, including depression, traumatic brain injury (TBI), and PTSD.

For those who develop PTSD, there is not a one size fits all approach. Treatment should be symptom-based and follow a three-pronged approach of psychoeducation, pharmacotherapy, and psychotherapy. Psychotherapy is very effective in bringing someone out of the grip of PTSD, especially when it is integrated with the Word of God and Prayer. Counseling brings comfort, change, and hope, meeting the needs of hurting people. Those with PTSD, let me encourage you to get counseling.

The Conservation in War

Now, the best way to prevent experiencing PTS or PTSD is mental preparation. As such, I want to suggest another cognitive tool to help you before the fight. I love acronyms. This one has helped me: **SECURE**

S – Sovereignty of God
E – Endure
C – Communicate
U – Understand
R – Reflect
E – Empower others

S – <u>Sovereignty of God</u>: There is an excellent scene in the Ridley Scott film *Kingdom of Heaven* which I believe makes a great point. A group of soldiers come to take Orlando Bloom's character Balian, who is wanted for killing a priest. It is the words of a German knight which I think best sums up the chivalric theology of that era. When told to give up Balian, the German says, "If you say he's guilty, then we'll fight, and God will decide the truth of it." This commendable expression which ascribes God as the Judge of all the earth put steel in the spines of medieval knights.

It is often argued whether the Christian soldier has any benefit over his nonbelieving companion. As argued by Jesse Gray:

For soldiers who have entered military service with a firm otherworldly faith, there is frequently little difficulty in continuing to regard death as they did before, and the violence all about they will strengthen, rather than weaken, their convictions. On the other hand, soldiers whose religious faith is chiefly this-worldly, that is, social ethical in content, often find war's destruction wreaking havoc on their beliefs. The otherworldly soldier may prudently seek to stay alive as long as the worldly one. Unless he is a fanatic, he tries to listen to inner commands before acting rationally. But the difference becomes apparent when the chances of surviving a given engagement are reduced and death becomes as nearly certain as it ever does in combat. Then such an otherworldly soldier rarely cringes from his fate, does not become despondent or bitterly reproachful of others. Inwardly he may be exultant or simply collected. What is coming has been determined by greater and wiser forces than he commands, and he is content to repeat: "Thy will be done," or its equivalent. We destroyers of such soldiers are astounded at how bravely they die and are sometimes deeply shaken by it. It seems to be contrary to nature but the steadfastness of that will which is fixed on a life beyond death can endure the pain of dying and sometimes achieve exaltation in the act.[11]

All this is to say, that the great warriors of the past have fortified themselves with a firm reliance on the protection of divine Providence, and a faith in the One who makes, and controls history.

E – Endure: Trauma is a natural reaction to an unnatural event. War is more traumatic than other forms of trauma for at least three reasons: Uncertainty, danger, and chance. Combat occurs within the realm of uncertainty as a fog of war shrouds the unknown. There are just so many variables and ways to be maimed and quartered by the hands of war. War also wounds the soul, never leaving us the same, so that "what protrudes and does not fit in our past rises to haunt us."[12]

For all of us who have experienced war, this is a call to endure for the sake of those we serve. God created us to

---

[11] J. Glenn Gray, *The Warriors: Reflections on Men in Battle* (New York: Bison, 1970), 119.
[12] *The Warriors*, 24.

be resilient, and with His help, we can overcome our greatest fears and succeed.

C – <u>Communicate</u>: Combat is arguably more traumatic than other forms of trauma for the simple fact that soldiers often suppress their feelings and accept that what they went through was expected for their line of work. This is true. A prominent trait of the warrior class is to repress trauma. However, trauma that festers can become dangerous. Trauma can be crippling and debilitating if left unchecked. A hurdle here is, most men do not communicate their feelings adequately. Acknowledging this, Carl Jung offers the following:

The emotion withheld is also something we conceal – something which we can hide even from ourselves – an art in which men particularly excel, while women, with very few exceptions, are by nature adverse to doing such violence to their emotions. When emotion is withheld it tends to isolate and disturb us quite as much as an unconscious secret and is equally guilt laden. Just as nature abhors a vacuum, in this respect, in the long run nothing is more unbearable than a tepid harmony in personal relations brought about by withholding emotion. The repressed emotions are often of a kind we wish to keep secret.[13]

However, there is great cathartic value in sharing trauma within a so-called circle of trust. The goal of catharsis is "not mere intellectual acknowledgement of the facts, but their confirmation by the heart and the

---

[13] Carl G. Jung, *Modern Man in Search of a Soul* (New York: Harvest, 1933), 34.

actual release of the suppressed emotions."[14] As a Christian, I would also advocate the healing power of the Word of God and prayer, surrendering our harmful emotions and thoughts to God and each other (James 5:16).

U – **Understand**: A large part of PTSD deals with fear and anxiety as traumatic memories are encoded emotionally. In his book, *The Body Keeps the Score*, psychologist Bessel Van der Kolk states, "As long as you keep secrets and suppress information, you are fundamentally at war with yourself. The critical issue is allowing yourself to know what you know. That takes an enormous amount of courage."[15] Understanding the nature of trauma, of how the body can keep the score, helps us to move on. The goal is to be free from the control of anxiety and fear. This means we reset ourselves mentally and emotionally whenever we experience harmful thoughts and feelings.

R – **Reflect**: According to Aristotle, all learning involves pain.[16] That may not fit all situations of life, but it certainly fits war. Reflecting on our pain helps us from bottling it up, or worse, treating it with drugs or alcohol. Reflecting and processing the traumatic event that happened to us gives it meaning. Something that has helped me immensely is the technique of writing.

---

[14] Ibid., 36.
[15] Bessel A. Van der Kolk, *The Body Keeps the Score: Brain, Mind, And Body in The Healing of Trauma* (New York: Penguin Books, 2015), 235.
[16] Aristotle, *Nicomachean Ethics*, Book V, 1.1301.

Author Jesse Gray experienced a measure of peace by journalling. His experiences in WWII led him once to write, "the deepest fear of my war years, one still with me, is that these happenings had no real purpose."[17] By journalling, Gray was able to give meaning to the trauma that rose up to haunt him. Likewise, the passage of time puts a new face on an old experience.

Another discipline that has paid immense dividends to me and scores of others is reading the accounts of warriors in their words. I don't mean mere hagiographic drivel. A good autobiography is honest and piercing. Besides, reading in general is important to stave off atrophy of the mind.

As the Russian juggernaut was bearing down on them, the German high command, anxious to assess the morale of their encircled soldiers at Stalingrad, sent word that the men could write letters home, and that mail would be forwarded to their homes by plane. Most of the men understood but this would more than likely be their last communication with those they loved. After the letters were written, they were collected and stored away, never being delivered to the addressees. Later discovered and published, these letters reveal much. The following is from a soldier who was a pianist:

Perhaps it is the will of destiny that our situation here has come to a point which permits no excuses and no way out. I do not know whether I shall have a chance to talk to you once more. So, it is well that this letter should reach you, and that you

---

[17] *The Warriors*, 24.

know, in case I should turn up some day, that my hands are ruined and have been since the beginning of December. I lost the little finger on my left hand, but worse still is the loss of the three middle fingers of my right hand through frostbite. I can hold my drinking cup only with my thumb and little finger. I am quite helpless; only when one has lost his fingers does one notice how much they are needed for the simplest tasks. The thing I can still do best with my little finger is shoot. Yes, my hands are wrecked. I can't very well spend the rest of my life shooting, simply because I'm no good for anything else. Perhaps I could make out as a game warden? But this is gallows humor; I only write it to calm myself.

The translated letter is from a German soldier who was an actor:

You are my witness that I never wanted to go along with it, because I was afraid of the East, in fact of war in general. I have never been a soldier, only a man in uniform. What do I get out of it? What do the others get out of it, those who went along and were not afraid? Yes, what are we getting out of it? We, who are playing the walk-on parts in this madness incarnate? What good does a hero's death do us? I have played death on the stage dozens of times, but I was only playing, and you sat out front in plush seats, and thought my acting authentic and realize how little the acting had to do with real death. You were supposed to die heroically, inspiringly, from inner conviction and for a great cause. But what is death in reality here? Here they croak, starve, freeze to death – it's nothing but a biological fact like eating and drinking. They drop like flies; nobody cares and nobody buries them. Without arms or legs and without eyes, with bellies around everywhere.

One should make a movie of it; it would make "the most beautiful death in the world" impossible once and for all. It is a death fit for beasts; later they will ennoble it on granite friezes showing "dying warriors" with bandages. Poems, novels, and hymns will be written and sung. And in the churches, they will say masses. I'll have no part of it, because I have no desire to rot in a mass grave. I have written the same thing to Professor H – . You and he will hear from me again. Don't be surprised if it takes a while, because I have decided to take my fate into my own hands.

These last letters from warriors hardly need a commentary. As I myself have learned, by journalling, I have giving meaning to many traumatic events I lived through and processed them. Such feelings can be intense and linger for years, even decades. Grief is a normal feeling that is triggered by loss. Journalling helps us tackle these traumatic twins.

E – <u>Empower others</u>: By these techniques, we can navigate through the wreckage of post-incident trauma to pick up the pieces of our lives and carry on in the fight. Those of us who have can then help others.

As Safe in Battle as I am in Bed

It was the wee hours of the morning on Sunday, March 25, 2006. Our Troop, of C Squadron, were conducting a raid on an Al-Qaeda operative in Abu Gharib, Iraq. Following a short drive down Route Irish, we hit our vehicle drop off (VDO) point then fanned out around the walled compound. It was a typical Iraqi house. A two-story, white plastered block building with a flat roof. Nothing in particular set it apart from the millions of others like it. We had hit many like this before. I set the ladder, that I was carrying, against the wall. Then, one by one, our team climbed into the courtyard. It was just after one in the morning on my thirty-sixth birthday. The other teams made their stealthy approach, then we paused and poised for the assault.

Then the countdown came, five, four, three, two, boom! The door charges belched their explosive residue into the night air, and we were in. We cleared our way through the house and entered the next to the last room. At that point, we had yet to find the man we had come to kill or capture. I posted security outside an open door. The guy behind me threw in a diversionary grenade. On the second "boom" I broke the threshold of the doorway. Seeing the wall, I took the unknown, turning ninety-degrees to clear the unseen part of the room. I had no sooner broke the threshold when I experienced something like getting hit in the head with a mallet. A second later, I was lying on my back looking up at the ceiling. The sound of the bullet reverberated between my ears. I had been shot in the throat just above the body armor, but it felt like I got shot in the head. In fact, my first thought was I no longer had a head.

Stunned and unable to move, I was waiting for the man who shot me to finish me off. It seemed like it would happen at any second. I would look up and see a gun barrel in my face, get a *coup de grâce*, then step over a dark threshold. Time slowed down. Within a few seconds, the rest of my team engaged the guy who shot me. Their bullets flung him back into yet another room, just beyond the one I was in. No sooner did a teammate drag me out of the room, then several grenades went off. My team was working on ending that guy. It all took seconds. As my team battled to eliminate the threat, I laid prostrate, keenly aware of my own mortality and transience. While my life seemed to be a mere breath away from that undiscovered country, I was suddenly engulfed with a fabulous warmth and peace that defies expression. The atmosphere around me became like that of heaven itself, dispelling the feeling of hovering death from my thoughts. In that moment of acceptance, as I anticipated what lie beyond, I was completely without fear and at rest. Then I went unconscious.

Unbeknownst to me at the time, my team had sent our bad guy to the next world and prepared me for medical evacuation. As Dave, my medic went to work on me, the truly remarkable part of this story is the path that bullet took. I had gotten shot a mere inch above my body armor. The bullet entered my tracheal notch, clipped my collar bone, then passed through my right shoulder. Normally, getting shot in the throat is a done deal, especially from a few feet away. At about nine hundred feet per second, the bullet entered my throat, head on, but was somehow redirected to about a forty-five-degree angle where it continued until exiting at my right shoulder. In the words of the Army surgeon at Walter Reed who spoke to my mother, "The bullet's path, could in no way be recreated even with the most modern sophisticated equipment." "I don't believe in God," said the surgeon, "but He surely delivered your son."

There is no doubt in my mind that I should have died that night, on my birthday. But I believe in the sovereignty of God; I was supernaturally preserved. I had gotten shot on my second trip to Iraq. The hard part was going back into harm's way the next three times. On my next trip, it seemed that every bullet was intended for me, and every bomb would likely land on my head. Wherever I went, it seemed death was ready to pounce. I had to get back to a good place in my mind and face the prospect of death with equanimity. I needed to get back to where I sensed the eternal in the immediate presence of death. I did that by having faith in the One who makes, and controls history. This enables me to be as safe in battle as I am in bed.

Moreover, all things being equal, I should have a lot of trauma. But by the grace of God, I don't. I know many who have PTSD, both believers and unbelievers. While I am not sure why some develop PTSD and others do not, I have recognized a trait in unbelievers with PTSD. What they did in combat doesn't seem to bode well with them. Something about their experience just doesn't sit well with their conscience. Some say this is because war is murder, and the Bible forbids murder. However, as I have tried to show in chapter two, the Bible forbids murder, which is illegal killing, but not killing. The point is, there is a distinction between killing and murder. Perhaps part of the reason some develop PTSD may be due to issues related to a troubled conscience?

As I have seen, most vets that experience posttraumatic issues take the self-medicate route and stuff their problems until things reach a breaking point. I have buried many that fall into this category. Exacerbating this issue, in the ranks, PTSD is considered weak. Because of this incorrect and prevalent stigma, it is extremely difficult to get people to open up, let alone seek treatment.

Though vets think therapy and the stigma of PTSD is weak, it's the truly courageous ones who seek help. As Carl Jung once put it, "we cannot change anything unless we accept it." The challenge is for us to remove the stigma of weakness from PTSD. Consider, when someone we have served with gets shot in the line of duty, there is no stigma, only honor. Why should there be dishonor involving the invisible wounds of war?

Having surveyed the underbelly of war, let it be said that combat is truly intense and is certainly the ultimate crucible. However, it's important to note that experiences in war don't always result in mental injury. In fact, the overwhelming majority of veterans may never experience PTS or PTSD. Moreover, we are not exactly sure why some things cause trauma in some but not others. The important thing is to prepare and condition our minds before the fight. This gives us the best chances of success.

Introspection

I have purposely bookended each chapter with five introspective questions. These are designed to promote professional growth:

1. Is there something from your past that haunts you?

2. Have you been through an event or experience that caused you to fear for your life?

3. Do you try to avoid people, places, things, or situations that remind you of what happened?

4. Are you struggling with negative emotions?

5. Are you struggling with unwanted behaviors?

The Surrender of Cornwallis at Yorktown, October 19, 1781.

8

Conclusion

"Nations have passed away and left no traces, and history gives the naked cause of it – one single, simple reason in all cases; they fell because their peoples were not fit." – Kipling

I began with the thought that as a Nation, we aren't where we used to be, or need to be in many ways. Even progressive news agencies are waking up. According to a January 29, 2023, NBC News poll, "America is a deeply pessimistic country that is distrustful of its own government with an overall outlook that is historically bleak." Over 70% of Americans believe our country is headed in the wrong direction. More than two-thirds use negative words and phrases to describe where we are: 'downhill,' 'wrong track,' 'disaster,' 'hard times,' and

206

'uncertain.' With over 70% of Americans saying that the Nation is on the wrong track, how important is it for those of us who defend society to return to first principles? The very future of America is at stake.

Earlier, I mentioned what the warrior philosopher Vegetius wrote about Rome in his day. He said, the decline and eventual fall of Rome was due primarily to the warrior class straying away from their ideals, that is, the warrior virtues. Now, if you ask me, the similarity between Vegetius' day and ours is obvious. Amidst our society's crumbling foundations, as guardians of the Republic, how important is it for us then to reemphasize the utmost importance of the warrior ethos, to reestablish an operating baseline of excellence, by reaffirming these warrior virtues as standards of excellence?! Because, as President Reagan once reminded us, "Freedom is never more than one generation away from extinction." As guardians of the republic, the American warrior class must recover the sense that we are the standard bearers of the virtues that hold our Nation together. The American warrior culture must be affirmed and sustained, as it maintains the Nation's existence.

As has been argued, the warrior class not only comes from our society, but its ranks also hold our society together. Every generation of warriors must therefore be reminded of these truths. We must recover our warrior culture. This will enable us to confront the various uncertainties that will no doubt come down the pike. By so doing, we will extoll the value of sacred honor. An ideal warrior is smart, strong, socially astute, but above all, is just in his dealings, and holds honor to be sacred. The only lasting thing in the world is the noble name one gains by living a life filled with noble deeds. Knowing and practicing these five warrior virtues enables us to conduct ourselves in such a way "that all men wish to be our friends and all fear to be our enemies."

I want to leave you with a thought: Wisdom is a journey, and life is a learning competition. I gained this idea from my multiple readings of Sun Tzu's *The Art of War*. Famously, Sun Tzu states, "Know the enemy and know yourself; in a hundred battles you will never be in peril. However, as he goes on to say, "If you know yourself but not the enemy, for every victory gained you will also suffer a defeat." In other words, if you only know yourself, but not your opponent, you may win or lose. Who knows. Further, he states, "If you know neither the enemy nor yourself, you will succumb in every battle," that is, you will be over-powered and destroyed. The point is, Sun Tzu put equal importance to both knowing our enemy and knowing ourselves. Life is a learning competition, and he who would move the world must first move himself.

Many go through life wondering if they will ever make an impact. A veteran should never have that problem. The greatest honor anyone can have is the opportunity to serve. This was true 2,000 years ago, its true today, and it'll be true tomorrow. In conclusion, let me leave you with a parting shot. One which I hope will encourage you to live up to the ideals of our great Nation. First, never forget your oath which includes the words, "I solemnly swear that I will support and defend the Constitution of the United States against all enemies, foreign and domestic." Second, remember that you are not irreplaceable. If you fail to live up to the great creeds and codes of the profession of arms, you will of necessity be rightly removed from these storied ranks. Third, find your worth in service. In light of the great privilege to serve, let it be said, the American people have every right to expect the very best from us. Great things have been done, but greater things are yet to be done! For those of us who have served, service to our great Nation is its own reward.

Truth, Strength, and Honor!

Introspection

I have purposely bookended each chapter with five introspective questions. These are designed to promote professional growth:

1. What do you value more than anything else?

2. What motivates you?

3. What are your goals?

4. How do you define success?

5. Has this book helped you?

Appendix A: The Ten Warrior Principles

Honor

1. Know: Sowing virtue, reaps honor.

2. Do: Be professional. Be polite. Be prepared to kill.

Integrity

3. Know: Integrity keeps honor intact.

4. Do: Do what is right, even to your own hurt.

Loyalty

5. Know: Duty is the privilege of service.

6. Do: Serve faithfully, even when it's not appreciated.

Temperance

7. Know: Temperance is mastery over instinct.

8. Do: Focus on what you can control.

Courage

9. Know: Courage is every virtue at its testing point.

10. Do: Sense danger but embrace it willingly.

Appendix B: American Warrior Philosophy

Virtue	Definition	Concept	Principles
HONOR	A sacred prize.	*Law of Honor*	1. Sowing virtue reaps honor. 2. Be professional. Be polite. Be prepared to kill.
INTEGRITY	A sacred trust.	*Moral Compass*	3. Integrity keeps honor intact. 4. Do what is right, even to your own hurt.
LOYALTY	A sacred bond.	*Brotherhood*	5. Duty is the privilege of service. 6. Serve faithfully, even when it's not appreciated.
TEMPERANCE	A quality that keeps us honorable.	*Dichotomy of Control*	7. Temperance is mastery over instinct. 8. Focus on what you can control.
COURAGE	A true sense of danger with a willingness to embrace it.	*Mental Resolve*	9. Courage is every virtue at its testing point. 10. Sense danger but embrace it willingly.

Appendix C: The Code of Conduct
(August 17, 1955)

Article I: I am an American fighting man. I serve in the forces which guard my country and our way of life. I am prepared to give my life in their defense.

Article II: I will never surrender of my own free will. If in command I will never surrender my men while they still have the means to resist.

Article III: If I am captured I will continue to resist by all means available. I will make every effort to escape and aid others to escape. I will accept neither parole nor special favors from the enemy.

Article IV: If I become a prisoner of war, I will keep faith with my fellow prisoners. I will give no information or take part in any action which might be harmful to my comrades. If I am senior, I will take command. If not, I will obey the lawful orders of those appointed over me and will back them up in every way.

Article V: When questioned, should I become a prisoner of war, I am bound to give only name, rank, service number, and date of birth. I will evade answering further questions to the utmost of my ability. I will make no oral or written statements disloyal to my country and its allies or harmful to their cause.

Article VI: I will never forget that I am an American fighting man, responsible for my actions, and dedicated to the principles which made my country free. I will trust in my God and in the United States of America.

Appendix D: Recommended Reading List

As the avid reader readily understands, reading offers ageless insights, wisdom, and methods that are often adaptable to one's current environment or situation. Through reading, one may gain 'theoretical experience,' a sort of imaginative practical application. In other words, by means of our conceptual and imaginative abilities, we may gain theoretical experience as though we had 'been there and done that' ourselves. In light of this, I offer you the following twenty-five books for your professional development:

1. The Mission, the Men, and Me –Blaber
2. The Quiet Professional – Hoe
3. Five Years to Freedom – Rowe
4. Triple Canopy – O'Kelley
5. The Art of War – Sun Tzu
6. Spec Ops – McRaven
7. Operation Jedburgh –Beavan
8. We Remained – Volckmann
9. Fire in the Jungle –Schmidt
10. MacArthur's Undercover War – Breuer
11. From OSS to Green Berets – Bank
12. The Secret War Against Hanoi –Shultz
13. SOG – Plaster
14. The Only Thing Worth Dying For – Blehm
15. Out of the Mountains – Kilcullen
16. The Accidental Guerrilla – Kilcullen
17. War of the Flea –Taber
18. On Guerrilla Warfare – Mao Tse-Tung
19. Learning to Eat Soup with a Knife – Nagl

20. Counterinsurgency Warfare: Theory and Practice – Galula
21. Survival Mindset – Crittenden
22. The Ugly American – Burdick
23. Tactical Leadership – LeFavor
24. The Wild Fields – LeFavor
25. #Fail: Why the US Lost the War in Afghanistan – Owen

Appendix E: Principles of War

Antoine Jomini believed there could be fundamental, almost mathematical principles of war which, stemming from the study and observation of Napoleonic warfare and strategy, could stand for all time.[1] As such, he observed, "There have existed in all times fundamental principles on which depend good results in warfare. These principles are unchanging, independent of the kind of weapons, of historical time and of place."[2] History agrees.

The principles of war may be memorized using the acronym: **MOOSE MUSS**

Maneuver – Place the enemy in a disadvantageous position through the flexible application of combat power.

Objective – Direct every military operation toward a clearly defined, decisive, and attainable objective.

Offensive – Seize, retain, and exploit the initiative. Pressure, pursue, and punish.

Surprise – Strike the enemy at a time or place or in a manner for which he is unprepared.

---

[1] As John Alger tells us, these principles have their distant roots in Baron Jomini's *The Art of War*, and their immediate roots in the work of Major General J.F.C. Fuller as he attempted to distill lessons from the failed British campaigns of 1914-1915.

[2] Jomini, Traité des Grandes Opérations Militaires, III, 333.

Appendix E: Principles of War

Economy of Force – Allocate minimum essential combat power to secondary efforts.

Mass – Concentrate the effects of combat power at the decisive place and time.

Unity of Command – For every objective, ensure unity of effort under one responsible commander.

Security – Never permit the enemy to acquire an unexpected advantage. Preserve your force as a whole.

Simplicity – Prepare clear, uncomplicated plans and clear, concise orders to ensure thorough understanding.

Appendix F: Principles of Leadership

1. <u>Be technically and tactically proficient</u>. Effective leaders are smart. They not only possess domain knowledge of their field of expertise and their own duties and responsibilities, but they know those of their team as well. Your proficiency will earn the respect of your team. Additionally, leaders must understand how best to employ the equipment and weaponry of their team in order to achieve success. This principle demands that leaders take responsibility for staying abreast of current military developments through training, experience, reading and study.

2. <u>Know yourself and seek self-improvement</u>. Professional development is a continuous process. An effective leader evaluates his strengths and weaknesses. Through self-evaluation, a leader is able to recognize his strengths and weaknesses. In this way he can determine his particular capabilities and limitations. As a result, he can take specific actions to further develop his strengths and work on correcting his weaknesses. This process builds self-confidence.

An accurate and clear understanding of yourself and a comprehension of group behavior will help you determine the best way to deal with any given situation. Leaders must be genuine. As Hawthorne so poignantly illustrates, "No man, for any considerable period, can wear one face to himself, and another to the multitude, without finally getting bewildered as to which may be the true." Be genuine and honest.

3. <u>Seek responsibility and take responsibility for your actions and decisions</u>. Achieving organizational results means accepting responsibility. Responsibility is demonstrated by decisiveness in times of crisis – not hesitating to make decisions or to act to achieve operational results. Seeking responsibilities also means taking responsibility for your actions. You are responsible for all your unit does or fails to do. Be willing to accept justified and constructive criticism.

4. <u>Know your men and look out for their well-being</u>. Leaders must know and understand those being led. When your men trust you, they will willingly work to accomplish any mission. Successful leaders know their men and how they react to different situations. This knowledge can save lives. Further, knowledge of your men's personalities will enable you, as the leader, to decide how best to employ each man.

5. <u>Keep your men informed</u>. Your subordinates expect to be kept informed, and when possible, have the reasons behind the requirements and decisions explained to them. Your men will perform better and, if knowledgeable of the situation, can carry on without your personal supervision. Providing information inspires initiative.

6. <u>Make sound and timely decisions</u>. Leaders must be able to reason under the most critical conditions. Rapidly estimate a situation and make a sound decision based on that estimation. There's no room for reluctance to make a decision. As MacArthur reminds "never give an order that

can't be obeyed." Likewise, subordinates respect the leader who corrects his mistakes immediately.

7. <u>Employ your team in accordance with its capabilities</u>. Successful completion of a task depends upon how well you know your men's capabilities. Good leaders seek out challenging tasks for their subordinates that they are not only prepared for, but have the ability to successfully complete the mission as well.

8. <u>Ensure each task is understood, supervised, and accomplished</u>. Good leaders communicate their instructions in a clear, concise manner, and allow their men a chance to ask questions. Leaders should also check progress periodically to confirm the assigned task is properly accomplished. This allows your men to know you are concerned about mission accomplishment as well as them.

9. <u>Develop a sense of responsibility in your subordinates</u>. Good leaders show subordinates they're interested in their welfare by giving them the opportunity for professional development. Assigning tasks and delegating authority promotes mutual confidence and respect between the leader and the men. The key element of trust, the fundamental bedrock in the relationship between the leader and the led, is fostered in this way.[1]

10. <u>Set the example</u>. No aspect of leadership is more powerful. Set the standards for your men by personal example. Your subordinates all watch your appearance,

---

[1] Kolenda, *Leadership: The Warrior's Art*, xxii.

attitude, physical fitness and personal example. If your personal standards are high, then you can rightfully demand the same of your men. Your personal example affects your subordinates more than any amount of instruction or form of discipline.

11. <u>Build a team</u>. A good leader is socially astute and understands that one must train your element with a purpose and emphasize the essential elements of teamwork and realism. Good leaders foster a team spirit that motivates subordinates to work with confidence and competence. As Clausewitz observes, "It is only by means of a great directing spirit that we can expect the full power latent in the troops to be developed" [2] Further, a good leader should always ensure that subordinates know their positions and responsibilities within the team framework.

12. <u>Create a positive climate</u>.[3] Good leaders understand that they set the moral and psychological thermostat in both battle and the workspace. This principle is relative to what is referred to in the military as 'presence.' This principle reminds us that good leaders galvanize the strengths of others. Thus, rather than seeing strengths in others a threat to our leadership, good leaders envision how to implement those strengths and motivate their subordinates to use them. Moreover, control and order are immediately reestablished by presence.[4] A critical

---

[2] Clausewitz, *On War*, I. 3.
[3] Historically there have been eleven principles. I have presumed to add this twelfth principle for the consideration of the military community.
[4] Taylor, *Military Leadership*, 36.

component of presence is composure, that is, a leader's command over himself.

Reading of the Declaration of Independence 1776.

Appendix G: The Declaration of Independence

Every American warrior takes an oath to uphold and defend the Constitution of the United States against all enemies foreign and domestic. It is therefore helpful to know and understand what we so swear.

IN CONGRESS, July 4, 1776.

The unanimous Declaration of the thirteen united States of America,

When in the Course of human events, it becomes necessary for one people to dissolve the political bands which have connected them with another, and to assume among the powers of the earth, the separate and equal station to which the Laws of Nature and of Nature's God entitle them, a decent respect to the opinions of mankind requires that they should declare the causes which impel them to the separation.

We hold these truths to be self-evident, that all men are created equal, that they are endowed by their Creator with certain unalienable Rights, that among these are Life, Liberty and the pursuit of Happiness. That to secure these rights, Governments are instituted among Men, deriving their just powers from the consent of the governed, --That whenever any Form of Government becomes destructive of these ends, it is the Right of the People to alter or to abolish it, and to institute new Government, laying its foundation on such principles and organizing its powers in such form, as to them shall seem most likely to effect their Safety and Happiness. Prudence, indeed, will dictate that Governments long established should not be changed for light and transient causes; and accordingly all experience hath shewn, that mankind are more disposed to suffer, while evils are sufferable, than to right themselves by abolishing the forms to which they are accustomed. But when a long train of abuses and usurpations, pursuing invariably the same Object evinces a design to reduce them under absolute Despotism, it is their right, it is their duty, to throw off such Government, and to provide new Guards for their future security.--Such has been the patient sufferance of these Colonies; and such is now the necessity which constrains them to alter their former Systems of Government. The history of the present King of Great Britain is a history of repeated injuries and usurpations, all having in direct object the establishment of an absolute Tyranny over these States. To prove this, let Facts be submitted to a candid world.

He has refused his Assent to Laws, the most wholesome and necessary for the public good.

He has forbidden his Governors to pass Laws of immediate and pressing importance, unless suspended in their operation till his Assent should be obtained; and when so suspended, he has utterly neglected to attend to them.

He has refused to pass other Laws for the accommodation of large districts of people, unless those people would relinquish the right of

Representation in the Legislature, a right inestimable to them and formidable to tyrants only.

He has called together legislative bodies at places unusual, uncomfortable, and distant from the depository of their public Records, for the sole purpose of fatiguing them into compliance with his measures.

He has dissolved Representative Houses repeatedly, for opposing with manly firmness his invasions on the rights of the people.

He has refused for a long time, after such dissolutions, to cause others to be elected; whereby the Legislative powers, incapable of Annihilation, have returned to the People at large for their exercise; the State remaining in the mean time exposed to all the dangers of invasion from without, and convulsions within.

He has endeavoured to prevent the population of these States; for that purpose obstructing the Laws for Naturalization of Foreigners; refusing to pass others to encourage their migrations hither, and raising the conditions of new Appropriations of Lands.

He has obstructed the Administration of Justice, by refusing his Assent to Laws for establishing Judiciary powers.

He has made Judges dependent on his Will alone, for the tenure of their offices, and the amount and payment of their salaries.

He has erected a multitude of New Offices, and sent hither swarms of Officers to harrass our people, and eat out their substance.

He has kept among us, in times of peace, Standing Armies without the Consent of our legislatures.

He has affected to render the Military independent of and superior to the Civil power.

He has combined with others to subject us to a jurisdiction foreign to our constitution, and unacknowledged by our laws; giving his Assent to their Acts of pretended Legislation:

For Quartering large bodies of armed troops among us:

For protecting them, by a mock Trial, from punishment for any Murders which they should commit on the Inhabitants of these States:

For cutting off our Trade with all parts of the world:

For imposing Taxes on us without our Consent:

For depriving us in many cases, of the benefits of Trial by Jury:

For transporting us beyond Seas to be tried for pretended offences

For abolishing the free System of English Laws in a neighbouring Province, establishing therein an Arbitrary government, and enlarging its Boundaries so as to render it at once an example and fit instrument for introducing the same absolute rule into these Colonies:

For taking away our Charters, abolishing our most valuable Laws, and altering fundamentally the Forms of our Governments:

For suspending our own Legislatures, and declaring themselves invested with power to legislate for us in all cases whatsoever.

He has abdicated Government here, by declaring us out of his Protection and waging War against us.

He has plundered our seas, ravaged our Coasts, burnt our towns, and destroyed the lives of our people.

He is at this time transporting large Armies of foreign Mercenaries to compleat the works of death, desolation and tyranny, already begun with circumstances of Cruelty

& perfidy scarcely paralleled in the most barbarous ages, and totally unworthy the Head of a civilized nation.

He has constrained our fellow Citizens taken Captive on the high Seas to bear Arms against their Country, to become the executioners of their friends and Brethren, or to fall themselves by their Hands.

He has excited domestic insurrections amongst us, and has endeavoured to bring on the inhabitants of our frontiers, the merciless Indian Savages, whose known rule of warfare, is an undistinguished destruction of all ages, sexes and conditions.

In every stage of these Oppressions We have Petitioned for Redress in the most humble terms: Our repeated Petitions have been answered only by repeated injury. A Prince whose character is thus marked by every act which may define a Tyrant, is unfit to be the ruler of a free people.

Nor have We been wanting in attentions to our Brittish brethren. We have warned them from time to time of attempts by their legislature to extend an unwarrantable jurisdiction over us. We have reminded them of the circumstances of our emigration and settlement here. We have appealed to their native justice and magnanimity, and we have conjured them by the ties of our common kindred to disavow these usurpations, which, would inevitably interrupt our connections and correspondence. They too have been deaf to the voice of justice and of consanguinity. We must, therefore, acquiesce in the necessity, which denounces our

Separation, and hold them, as we hold the rest of mankind, Enemies in War, in Peace Friends.

We, therefore, the Representatives of the united States of America, in General Congress, Assembled, appealing to the Supreme Judge of the world for the rectitude of our intentions, do, in the Name, and by Authority of the good People of these Colonies, solemnly publish and declare, That these United Colonies are, and of Right ought to be Free and Independent States; that they are Absolved from all Allegiance to the British Crown, and that all political connection between them and the State of Great Britain, is and ought to be totally dissolved; and that as Free and Independent States, they have full Power to levy War, conclude Peace, contract Alliances, establish Commerce, and to do all other Acts and Things which Independent States may of right do. **And for the support of this Declaration, with a firm reliance on the protection of divine Providence, we mutually pledge to each other our Lives, our Fortunes and our sacred Honor.**

The Five Warrior Virtues

Column 1	Column 2	Column 2 (Cont.)
Georgia:	North Carolina:	South Carolina:
Button Gwinnett	William Hooper	Edward Rutledge
Lyman Hall	Joseph Hewes	Thomas Heyward, Jr.
George Walton	John Penn	Thomas Lynch, Jr.
Arthur Middleton		

Column 3	Column 4	Column 5
Massachusetts:	Pennsylvania:	New York:
John Hancock	Robert Morris	William Floyd
	Benjamin Rush	Philip Livingston
Maryland:	Benjamin Franklin	Francis Lewis
Samuel Chase	John Morton	Lewis Morris
William Paca	George Clymer	
Thomas Stone	James Smith	
Charles Carroll	George Taylor	New Jersey:
	James Wilson	Richard Stockton
	George Ross	John Witherspoon
Virginia:		Francis Hopkinson
George Wythe		John Hart
Richard Henry Lee	Delaware:	Abraham Clark
Thomas Jefferson	Caesar Rodney	
Benjamin Harrison	George Read	
Thomas Nelson, Jr.	Thomas McKean	
Francis Lightfoot Lee		
Carter Braxton		

Column 6	Column 6 (Cont.)	Column 6 (Cont.)
New Hampshire:	Rhode Island:	New Hampshire:
Josiah Bartlett	Stephen Hopkins	Matthew Thornton
William Whipple	William Ellery	
Massachusetts:	Connecticut:	
Samuel Adams	Roger Sherman	
John Adams	Samuel Huntington	
Robert Treat Paine	William Williams	
Elbridge Gerry	Oliver Wolcott	

Appendix H: *American Crisis*
By Thomas Paine

THESE are the times that try men's souls. The summer soldier and the sunshine patriot will, in this crisis, shrink from the service of their country; but he that stands by it now, deserves the love and thanks of man and woman. Tyranny, like hell, is not easily conquered; yet we have this consolation with us, that the harder the conflict, the more glorious the triumph. What we obtain too cheap, we esteem too lightly: it is dearness only that gives everything its value. Heaven knows how to put a proper price upon its goods; and it would be strange indeed if so celestial an article as FREEDOM should not be highly rated. Britain, with an army to enforce her tyranny, has declared that she has a right (not only to TAX) but "to BIND us in ALL CASES WHATSOEVER" and if being bound in that manner, is not slavery, then is there not such a thing as slavery upon earth. Even the expression is impious; for so unlimited a power can belong only to God.

Whether the independence of the continent was declared too soon, or delayed too long, I will not now enter into as an argument; my own simple opinion is, that had it been eight months earlier, it would have been much better. We did not make a proper use of last winter, neither could we, while we were in a dependent state. However, the fault, if it were one, was all our own [NOTE]; we have none to blame but ourselves. But no great deal is lost yet. All that Howe has been doing for this month past, is rather a ravage than a conquest, which the

231

spirit of the Jerseys, a year ago, would have quickly repulsed, and which time and a little resolution will soon recover.

I have as little superstition in me as any man living, but my secret opinion has ever been, and still is, that God Almighty will not give up a people to military destruction, or leave them unsupportedly to perish, who have so earnestly and so repeatedly sought to avoid the calamities of war, by every decent method which wisdom could invent. Neither have I so much of the infidel in me, as to suppose that He has relinquished the government of the world, and given us up to the care of devils; and as I do not, I cannot see on what grounds the king of Britain can look up to heaven for help against us: a common murderer, a highwayman, or a house-breaker, has as good a pretense as he.

Tis surprising to see how rapidly a panic will sometimes run through a country. All nations and ages have been subject to them. Britain has trembled like an ague at the report of a French fleet of flat-bottomed boats; and in the fourteenth [fifteenth] century the whole English army, after ravaging the kingdom of France, was driven back like men petrified with fear; and this brave exploit was performed by a few broken forces collected and headed by a woman, Joan of Arc. Would that heaven might inspire some Jersey maid to spirit up her countrymen, and save her fair fellow sufferers from ravage and ravishment! Yet panics, in some cases, have their uses; they produce as much good as hurt. Their duration is always short; the mind soon grows through them, and acquires a firmer habit than before. But their peculiar advantage is, that they are the touchstones of sincerity and hypocrisy, and bring things and men to light, which might otherwise have lain forever undiscovered. In fact, they have the same effect on secret traitors, which an imaginary apparition would have upon a private murderer. They sift out the hidden thoughts of man, and hold them up in public to the world. Many a disguised Tory has lately shown his head, that shall penitentially solemnize with curses the day on which Howe arrived upon the Delaware.

As I was with the troops at Fort Lee, and marched with them to the edge of Pennsylvania, I am well acquainted with many circumstances, which those who live at a distance know but little or nothing of. Our situation there was exceedingly cramped, the place being a narrow neck of land between the North River and the Hackensack. Our force was inconsiderable, being not one-fourth so great as Howe could bring against us. We had no army at hand to have relieved the garrison, had we shut ourselves up and stood on our defense. Our ammunition, light artillery, and the best part of our stores, had been removed, on the apprehension that Howe would endeavor to penetrate the Jerseys, in which case Fort Lee could be of no use to us; for it must occur to every thinking man, whether in the army or not, that these kind of field forts are only for temporary purposes, and last in use no longer than the enemy directs his force against the particular object which such forts are raised to defend. Such was our situation and condition at Fort Lee on the morning of the 20th of November, when an officer arrived with information that the enemy with 200 boats had landed about seven miles above; Major General [Nathaniel] Green, who commanded the garrison, immediately ordered them under arms, and sent express to General Washington at the town of Hackensack, distant by the way of the ferry = six miles. Our first object was to secure the bridge over the Hackensack, which laid up the river between the enemy and us, about six miles from us, and three from them. General Washington arrived in about three-quarters of an hour, and marched at the head of the troops towards the bridge, which place I expected we should have a brush for; however, they did not choose to dispute it with us, and the greatest part of our troops went over the bridge, the rest over the ferry, except some which passed at a mill on a small creek, between the bridge and the ferry, and made their way through some marshy grounds up to the town of Hackensack, and there passed the river. We brought off as much baggage as the wagons could contain, the rest was lost. The simple object was to bring off the garrison, and march them on till they could be strengthened by the Jersey or Pennsylvania militia, so as to be enabled to make a stand. We staid four days at Newark, collected our out-posts with some of the Jersey militia, and marched out twice to meet the enemy, on being informed that they were advancing, though our numbers were greatly inferior to theirs. Howe, in my little opinion, committed a great error in generalship in not throwing a body of forces off from Staten Island through Amboy, by which means he might have seized all our stores at Brunswick, and intercepted our march into Pennsylvania; but if we believe the power of hell to be limited, we must likewise believe that their agents are under some providential control.

I shall not now attempt to give all the particulars of our retreat to the Delaware; suffice it for the present to say, that both officers and men, though greatly harassed and fatigued, frequently without rest, covering, or provision, the inevitable consequences of a long retreat, bore it with a manly and martial spirit. All their wishes centered in one, which was, that the country would turn out and help them to drive the enemy back. Voltaire has remarked that King William never appeared to full advantage but in difficulties and in action; the same remark may be made on General Washington, for the character fits him. There is a natural firmness in some minds which cannot be unlocked by trifles, but which, when unlocked, discovers a cabinet of fortitude; and I reckon it among those kind of public blessings, which we do not immediately see, that God hath blessed him with uninterrupted health, and given him a mind that can even flourish upon care.

I shall conclude this paper with some miscellaneous remarks on the state of our affairs; and shall begin with asking the following question, Why is it that the enemy have left the New England provinces, and made these middle ones the seat of war? The answer is easy: New England is not infested with Tories, and we are. I have been tender in raising the cry against these men, and used numberless arguments to show them their danger, but it will not do to sacrifice a world either to their folly or their baseness. The period is now arrived, in which either they or we must change our sentiments, or one or both must fall. And what is a Tory? Good God! What is he? I should not be afraid to go with a hundred Whigs against a thousand Tories, were they to attempt to get into arms. Every Tory is a coward; for servile, slavish, self-interested fear is the foundation of Toryism; and a man under such influence, though he may be cruel, never can be brave.

But, before the line of irrecoverable separation be drawn between us, let us reason the matter together: Your conduct is an invitation to the enemy, yet not one in a thousand of you has heart enough to join him. Howe is as much deceived by you as the American cause is injured by you. He expects you will all take up arms, and flock to his standard, with muskets on your shoulders. Your opinions are of no use to him, unless you support him personally, for 'tis soldiers, and not Tories, that he wants.

I once felt all that kind of anger, which a man ought to feel, against the mean principles that are held by the Tories: a noted one, who kept a tavern at Amboy, was standing at his door, with as pretty a child in his hand, about eight or nine years old, as I ever saw, and after speaking his mind as freely as he thought was prudent, finished with this unfatherly expression, "Well! give me peace in my day." Not a man lives on the continent but fully believes that a separation must some time or other finally take place, and a generous parent should have said, "If there must be trouble, let it be in my day, that my child may have peace;" and this single reflection, well applied, is sufficient to awaken every man to duty. Not a place upon earth might be so happy as America. Her situation is remote from all the wrangling world, and she has nothing to do but to trade with them. A man can distinguish himself between temper and principle, and I am as confident, as I am that God governs the world, that America will never be happy till she gets clear of foreign dominion. Wars, without ceasing, will break out till that period arrives, and the continent must in the end be conqueror; for though the flame of liberty may sometimes cease to shine, the coal can never expire.

America did not, nor does not want force; but she wanted a proper application of that force. Wisdom is not the purchase of a day, and it is no wonder that we should err at the first setting off. From an excess of tenderness, we were unwilling to raise an army, and trusted our cause to the temporary defense of a well-meaning militia. A summer's experience has now taught us better; yet with those troops, while they were collected, we were able to set bounds to the progress of the enemy, and, thank God! they are again assembling. I always considered militia as the best troops in the world for a sudden exertion, but they will not do for a long campaign. Howe, it is probable, will make an attempt on this city [Philadelphia]; should he fail on this side the Delaware, he is ruined. If he succeeds, our cause is not ruined. He stakes all on his side against a part on ours; admitting he succeeds, the consequence will be, that armies from both ends of the continent will march to assist their suffering friends in the middle states; for he cannot go everywhere, it is impossible. I consider Howe as the greatest enemy the Tories have; he is bringing a war into their country, which, had it not been for him and partly for themselves, they had been clear of. Should he now be expelled, I wish with all the devotion of a Christian, that the names of Whig and Tory may never more be mentioned; but should the Tories give him encouragement to come, or assistance if he come, I as sincerely wish that our next year's arms may expel them from the continent, and the Congress appropriate their possessions to the relief of those who have suffered in well-doing. A single successful battle next year will settle the whole. America could carry on a two years' war by the confiscation of the property of disaffected persons, and be made happy by their expulsion. Say not that this is revenge, call it rather the soft resentment of a suffering people, who, having no object in view but the good of all, have staked their own all upon a seemingly doubtful event. Yet it is folly to argue against determined hardness; eloquence may strike the ear, and the language of sorrow draw forth the tear of compassion, but nothing can reach the heart that is steeled with prejudice.

Quitting this class of men, I turn with the warm ardor of a friend to those who have nobly stood, and are yet determined to stand the matter out: I call not upon a few, but upon all: not on this state or that state, but on every state: up and help us; lay your shoulders to the wheel; better have too much force than too little, when so great an object is at stake. Let it be told to the future world, that in the depth of winter, when nothing but hope and virtue could survive, that the city and the country, alarmed at one common danger, came forth to meet and to repulse it. Say not that thousands are gone, turn out your tens of thousands; throw not the burden of the day upon Providence, but "show your faith by your works," that God may bless you. It matters not where you live, or what rank of life you hold, the evil or the blessing will reach you all. The far and the near, the home counties and the back, the rich and the poor, will suffer or rejoice alike. The heart that feels not now is dead; the blood of his children will curse his cowardice, who shrinks back at a time when a little might have saved the whole, and made them happy. I love the man that can smile in trouble, that can gather strength from distress, and grow brave by reflection. 'Tis the business of little minds to shrink; but he whose heart is firm, and whose conscience approves his conduct, will pursue his principles unto death. My own line of reasoning is to myself as straight and clear as a ray of light. Not all the treasures of the world, so far as I believe, could have induced me to support an offensive war, for I think it murder; but if a thief breaks into my house, burns and destroys my property, and kills or threatens to kill me, or those that are in it, and to "bind me in all cases whatsoever" to his absolute will, am I to suffer it? What signifies it to me, whether he who does it is a king or a common man; my countryman or not my countryman; whether it be done by an individual villain, or an army of them? If we reason to the root of things we shall find no difference; neither can any just cause be assigned why we should punish in the one case and pardon in the other.

Let them call me rebel and welcome, I feel no concern from it; but I should suffer the misery of devils, were I to make a whore of my soul by swearing allegiance to one whose character is that of a sottish, stupid, stubborn, worthless, brutish man. I conceive likewise a horrid idea in receiving mercy from a being, who at the last day shall be shrieking to the rocks and mountains to cover him, and fleeing with terror from the orphan, the widow, and the slain of America.

There are cases which cannot be overdone by language, and this is one. There are persons, too, who see not the full extent of the evil which threatens them; they solace themselves with hopes that the enemy, if he succeed, will be merciful. It is the madness of folly, to expect mercy from those who have refused to do justice; and even mercy, where conquest is the object, is only a trick of war; the cunning of the fox is as murderous as the violence of the wolf, and we ought to guard equally against both. Howe's first object is, partly by threats and partly by promises, to terrify or seduce the people to deliver up their arms and receive mercy. The ministry recommended the same plan to Gage, and this is what the tories call making their peace, "a peace which passeth all understanding" indeed! A peace which would be the immediate forerunner of a worse ruin than any we have yet thought of. Ye men of Pennsylvania, do reason upon these things! Were the back counties to give up their arms, they would fall an easy prey to the Indians, who are all armed: this perhaps is what some Tories would not be sorry for. Were the home counties to deliver up their arms, they would be exposed to the resentment of the back counties who would then have it in their power to chastise their defection at pleasure. And were any one state to give up its arms, that state must be garrisoned by all Howe's army of Britons and Hessians to preserve it from the anger of the rest. Mutual fear is the principal link in the chain of mutual love, and woe be to that state that breaks the compact. Howe is mercifully inviting you to barbarous destruction, and men must be either rogues or fools that will not see it. I dwell not upon the vapors of imagination; I bring reason to your ears, and, in language as plain as A, B, C, hold up truth to your eyes.

I thank God, that I fear not. I see no real cause for fear. I know our situation well, and can see the way out of it. While our army was collected, Howe dared not risk a battle; and it is no credit to him that he decamped from the White Plains, and waited a mean opportunity to ravage the defenseless Jerseys; but it is great credit to us, that, with a handful of men, we sustained an orderly retreat for near an hundred miles, brought off our ammunition, all our field pieces, the greatest part of our stores, and had four rivers to pass. None can say that our retreat was precipitate, for we were near three weeks in performing it, that the country might have time to come in. Twice we marched back to meet the enemy, and remained out till dark. The sign of fear was not seen in our camp, and had not some of the cowardly and disaffected inhabitants spread false alarms through the country, the Jerseys had never been ravaged. Once more we are again collected and collecting; our new army at both ends of the continent is recruiting fast, and we shall be able to open the next campaign with sixty thousand men, well armed and clothed. This is our situation, and who will may know it. By perseverance and fortitude we have the prospect of a glorious issue; by cowardice and submission, the sad choice of a variety of evils - a ravaged country - a depopulated city - habitations without safety, and slavery without hope - our homes turned into barracks and bawdy-houses for Hessians, and a future race to provide for, whose fathers we shall doubt of. Look on this picture and weep over it! and if there yet remains one thoughtless wretch who believes it not, let him suffer it unlamented.

December 23, 1776

About the Author

Paul D. LeFavor was born in Virginia and was raised in a pastor's family. He graduated from Liberty University and received his M.A. in Religion from Reformed Theological Seminary and his M.Div. from Liberty Theological Seminary. Paul retired from the US Army Special Forces in 2009, is married to Becky, his wife of twenty-seven years, and has two daughters Liane and Collette, and a granddaughter Annabel. He has served as the pastor of Christ Covenant Baptist Church, Fayetteville, North Carolina since 2012 and is the author of seven books, including the *US Army Small Unit Tactics Handbook*, *Tactical Leadership*, and *The Wild Fields: A Fight for the Soul of Ukraine*.

Index

Index

Connect with Blacksmith Publishing

www.thepinelander.com

www.blacksmithpublishingcom